"A page-turner crafted by a skillful storyteller . . . a welcome invitation to peek under the tent in academia to view a lifetime of reflections on very revealing male friendships. Peppered with humor and the mind of a foodie, Epstein shares the exhilarating highs experienced by faculty colleagues, lifetime friends, and family members . . . and the regret-filled lows of two divorces and missed opportunities to say goodbye in the midst of deeply held friendships."

—Michael J. Austin, Mack Professor Emeritus, University of California, Berkeley, Editor of *Social Justice and Social Work: Rediscovering a Core Value of the Profession*

"Having worked professionally with [Epstein] for years as a researcher, this book cements his legacy as a storyteller but takes it to a whole new level. I laughed, I cried, I spent some moments thinking about some of the significant relationships in my life. It's a warm, caring, thought-provoking look back at important relationships in one's life and why we seem drawn to some and not others. A book that offers important lessons about significant relationships no matter one's gender or sexual orientation."

—Paul Neitman, MSW, Children's Services Consultant

"Wonderfully candid, intriguing, and beautiful. The writing is superb, wit and insight impressive."

—Stuart Kirk, Professor Emeritus, UCLA, Author of *Revved*

"A raconteur of true grace and intelligence, Irwin Epstein shares his deep understanding of the human condition to bring new richness to the meaning of love and friendship. A delightful read for any man or woman."

—Cynthia Hayes, Author of *The Big Ordeal: Understanding and Managing the Psychological Turmoil of Cancer*

"Sad, funny, witty, thought provoking."

—Carol Ostrove

"Witty, erudite, thoughtful."

—Dana Holman, DSW

"A wonderful memoir. Irwin Epstein chose to write about his male friends and colleagues, but in exploring and revisiting those relationships in depth, his own life story emerges. His intelligence, impressive academic credentials, and his decades of teaching around the world, writing, and publishing give him a unique ability to see qualities in his subjects that others might miss. His extraordinary memory provides details from decades ago that give his subjects substance. . . . [T]hey are real, more than words on a page. Ultimately, what emerges is his interests, his character and sense of humor, his delight in food and neckties, and his consistent commitment to these friends that he cared about and loved."

—John Schiff, Architect

"The past sixty years have seen radical changes in the roles and expectations of men in our society. In this engaging book, which reads like a letter to a friend, sociologist and social-work researcher Irwin Epstein explores what it's been like for him to be a man in the twentieth and twenty-first centuries through his loving and not-so-loving recollections of male friends and the way each of them has affected his life. Flawed though they all are, you can't help wishing you'd known each of them. This is an honest yet witty reflection by an admittedly imperfect, hopefully non-misogynist, and by chance alone heterosexual man on what it's been like to be a man, an academic, and a single father in the tumultuous environment of the late twentieth and early twenty-first centuries. Not just for men alone, it indirectly encourages women to rethink the meaning of gender, friendship, and the way they live in their lives as well."

—Jane Miller, MSW, PhD, Author of *Seventy-Five Years of Social Work in Health Care in Melbourne, Australia*

"Memoirs are a sojourn into the past for idiosyncratic reasons. Undergirding this tricky passage are attempts to gain in-depth perspective and to reach fulfilling closure. Irwin Epstein's memoir not only arrives at both places but in this beautifully and lively written work adds to the particular genre by focusing almost exclusively on male time. His desire is to answer the puzzling question as to why and how he established loving, nonsexual, bonded relationships with certain men and not others. And so the overall effect is the unraveling of an autobiographical mystery, and ultimately the mastery of this extraordinary life."

—Joseph Boskin, Emeritus Professor, American Social History and African American Studies Boston University, Author of *Rebellious Laughter*

"Everyone has a story. Every story has its mark on historical times. Therefore, each story is both personal and public. I often tell my students that a social worker is no different from the clients; he is a person in society and history, shaped and oppressed by the values and consciousness of society. If social workers themselves cannot see the causes of these oppressions and injuries and break free from the shackles of mainstream ideology and culture, how can we have the strength to help others? How can we extradite others out of the darkness? How can we heal other people's wounds? . . . May God bless Irwin's new book!"

—Professor Ku, Hok Bun, PhD, Associate Professor of Social Service, Polytechnic University of Hong Kong

"Irwin's lifetime adventures with male friends are happily peppered with irony and often result in outright laughter. *Men as Friends* was a pleasure for this woman to read."

—Nancy B. Austin, PsyD, Psychologist

"So well composed and written. I have always appreciated my guy friends but haven't spent time reading and thinking about the relationship aspect of those friendships. Now I will. Congratulations on a timely work of art."

—Louis Siegelman, DDS

"Most commonly my 'beach read' is a book that is an easy read and soon forgotten. This is not that. It reminded me of a memoir I read over thirty years ago: *Tuesdays with Morrie* (Mitch Albom)."

—Donna Malwitz, Middle-School Nurse

"Irwin Epstein had a long career and built an international reputation as an academic researcher who wrote books and articles on professionalization and applied social work research in health and mental health among other subjects. Whatever the topic, he also always wrote with wit, fluidity, and great insight. In this memoir about the friends he loved and those that he was unable to, all his writing skill and psychological perceptiveness become central. Friendship, like love, is not always easy to understand, but Epstein writes with the kind of attention to complexity and empathy that makes this memoir unique."

—Leonard Quart, Author, Film Critic

"A thoughtfully rendered gallery of portraits of men that Epstein loved and a few he couldn't. The writing is crisp and witty but with the serious intention of getting at what turns friendship among men into love. A slow but I think discriminating reader, I don't get past page 10 in 50 percent of the books I start and quit another 25 percent somewhere in the middle. I actually finished this book! . . . [E]asy and satisfying read, no superfluous verbiage anywhere."

—George Roper, Artist, Fabric Designer

"The book reminded me to reach out to several classmates and friends I had as a kid in high school—people I haven't spoken to in years. Some were happy to hear from me. Some were cautious, but still pleasant. They need to read this book. All of us need books like this."

—Tony Stakis, Gothic Cabinet Craft

"Epstein's book is so vivid, so exquisite at times, that it feels more like observing Scorsese's film *My Voyage to Italy* than reading a memoir. But his voyages go beyond Rome in time and space. Boyhood, family, friendships found and lost—the author's subjectivity takes us along on a deeply personal voyage. To this Australian reader, it is cinematographic in its colorful detail."

—Sarah Jones, Psychotherapist, Author

"This is a book that transcends the personal and the professional while wittily and poignantly evoking the meaning of what is true closeness between male colleagues and friends. It is a joy to read and ponder."

—Ami Gantt, MSW, PhD, Adjunct Professor, Mount Sinai Medical Center

"I read this book during those quiet and uninterrupted blocks of time that are few and far between in my life. I took longer so I could focus. It's good. Really good. The writing is extremely witty, sardonic at times, wickedly intelligent. . . .

"If it were fiction, I would say that the 'character development' was top notch. The writing injects pathos into the hearts of readers through its many and varied stories. The men described, however, were/are real, not invented. All but one of them have passed, and that saddened me deeply. . . .

"The hindsight and reflection are remarkable and insightful. . . . It's what makes the book so personal, so powerful, and unique. This book needs to get out there in the world."

—Carol Segal, Dancer, Personal Trainer, Writer

"Initially, I anticipated a more scholarly, qualitative analysis of the book's key messages towards the end—some guidance for living a 'good life' amongst men friends. I was delighted that this was not the case. So many of we emeritus professors feel obliged to chisel in stone or print our own 'commandments' or sermons. This book is so much the better for just telling the story as it is and allowing readers to make our own reflections and derive our own learnings. It was elegant in its simplicity and profoundly impactful . . . without any overlaying pretentiousness or apparently wise self-commentary. The narrative was written in the manner of a master storyteller. Implied rather than imposed wisdom. Joyful but at the same time jolting. As a reader, I found myself going back to read sections over again to try and distill the important implications for my own life. Having enjoyed the first, often humor-filled read, I was compelled to return to understand and examine the complexities through the lens of my own life experiences more deeply. Thank you, good friend. Go well."

—Glenn Bowes, Professor Emeritus, University of Melbourne, Royal Children's Hospital

"Although Epstein distinguishes loving male relationships from homosexual unions, his book presents us with a reverie that is uncommon in its intimacy with men of his generation. This memoir uncovers the roots of his passion, from a turbulent, pathological, and patriarchal family propelling him into an distinguished intellectual career of research focusing on caring for people of all stripes and without judgment. The book is a compelling cultural and intellectual exploration of a life lived."

—Robert F. Carr, DSW, Psychoanalyst

"A great read. A researcher has written a memoir that reads like a novel. This is a book about deep friendships and how they do and don't develop. We learn about the author's family and how family dynamics produced a sensitive, caring individual, then an academic sociologist and social-work researcher who managed to remain a caring individual. Predictably, most of his friendships are men who are occupationally related and offer insights about how institutional demands and concerns influenced those relationships. When the researcher occasionally and inevitably emerges, research issues are explained succinctly and simply enough for the layperson to understand. But while the book is largely about male friendships in an academic context, it mirrors lives of men and women in offices, stores, factories, etc.

"The majority of individuals described in the book are no longer alive, continue to be missed by the author, but have been brought back to vibrant literary if not literal life for those of us who didn't know them but now wish we had."

—Jim Fogarty, Psychologist

"This is a diverse and compelling tale of Epstein's experiences with men that he came to love and cherish as friends and fellow travelers. Readers are offered a unique insight into how the protections afforded by one's family of origin and cultural heritage are also constraints that can be transcended if we open ourselves to others and let them matter to us. The men who are waiting to be discovered in these pages all matter to Irwin, and he let himself matter to them. . . . The author's natural curiosity, honest self-appraisal and attention to detail come together to produce a tender and often humorous rendering of a life well lived—so fortunate for the influence of friends and the blessing of being known and loved."

—Andrew Bruun, CEO, Youth Support and Advocacy Service, Melbourne, Australia

"In literary history, the genre called the essay is a relatively new form. After a lifetime of publishing purely academic prose, I was delighted to read Irwin Epstein's new book, *Men as Friends: From Cicero to Svevo to Cataldo*. Well laced with humor, psychological insight, and sociological awareness, his new book is a collection of individual tales that can be read as stand-alone essays, reflecting his experiences with men over the course of his life—some family, some boyhood pals, some professional, and many a combination of the personal and professional. In part a series of meditations on the joys and sorrows of friendships between men, Men as Friends lives up to its name. At times tender and funny and at times tough and critical, each chapter remains a thoroughly enjoyable read. Cumulatively, they present us with the half-life of a remarkably erudite, discerningly critical, often hilarious, and very loving man."

—Bruce A. Thyer, PhD, Distinguished Research Professor, Florida State University, College of Social Work

"A wonderful book, satisfying at every level. All of the principal inhabitants of the book (whether loved or not) were, on the page, absorbing characters. . . .

"[W]hat I find impressive . . . is the great range of experience [this book] encompasses, experience facilitated by . . . openness to seemingly every opportunity that came his way, whether prompted by a sabbatical, a divorce, or simply some sort of encounter from out of the blue. . . .

"But what I most appreciated about the book was simply the artfulness of its construction—not just at the level of the sentence or paragraph, but the book's overall shape. For me, it was a great source of aesthetic pleasure."

—Fritz Gaenslen, PhD, Professor Emeritus, Political Science and Asian Studies, Gettysburg College

"Reading Irwin's new book immediately brought to mind my father, who passed away twenty years ago. Despite the fact that he was restrained in emotional expression, his love and kindness have always been strongly felt, even up till now.

"Ancient Chinese philosopher Zhuangzi . . . has a famous saying, 'The friendship between gentlemen is as light as water.' . . . Generations after generations, these social expectations of the relationship between men have been firmly planted in the egos and superegos of many Chinese men and women. However, deep inside our ids, our urge for closeness is no different from anyone, anywhere in the world. . . .

"Irwin's book is truly enlightening! . . . Why can't 'gentlemen' . . . be more expressive of their feelings toward each other? Why can't we be truer to our ids or unconscious selves? I wholeheartedly thank Irwin for generously sharing his deep reflections and insightful understanding of his friendships with other men. I highly recommend this book to men of all ages and all cultures. And I highly recommend it to women who are interested in knowing another side of men."

—Siu-man Ng, PhD, Professor, Department of Social Work and Social Administration, University of Hong Kong

"A unique book! No one has undertaken such an effort. There is such a need for this book, and [Epstein] has addressed it so well. Though covering some rough terrain, it's extraordinarily readable, making the stories so much more insightful and useful. The only gap in the book is his secret guide to us all in being a *mensch*."

—William Cabin, PhD, Board of Directors, The Wellspring Congregation

"This book refreshed precious memories with Irwin, my PhD dissertation mentor. We met in Hong Kong, and I was studying what constituted a 'good death' for cancer patients. Our conversation was about death and bereavement. I shared with him my views and said, 'Good enough is enough.' Irwin smiled and responded, "Wallace, no. Good enough is not just enough; good enough is actually good.' . . . I will never forget that conversation. I congratulate Irwin on his good work."

—Wallace Chan, PhD, Associate Professor, Department of Social Work, Education and Community Wellbeing, Northumbria University, UK

"In his beautifully written, emotionally probing, and often hilarious exploration of his enduring and significant relationships with men, Irwin Epstein explores the bonds, affectionate and fraught, that have influenced and sustained him throughout life. With compassion and humor, Epstein chronicles the support, rivalry, identification, antagonism, and love that have characterized his male friendships and offers up a striking and complex portrait of masculinity. In his skillful telling, Irwin Epstein's memoir of friendship also serves as a partial autobiography, a reckoning with later age and how friendships with men have enriched and shaped his life's journey. Congratulations on climbing the Everest of writing this deeply personal and moving book."

—Jeffrey Harper, Author of *Please Cooperate: A Comedy of Bad Manners and A Few Thoughts from a Small Life*

"A beautifully composed memoir, richly describing his most important male relationships. Poignant, witty, and soulful."

—Fiona Eisenberg, PhD, LCSW, Psychotherapist

"Insightful, nuanced, challenging, thought-provoking. Irwin is an international treasure."

—Jerrold Jackson, PhD, Head of Machine Learning and Data, EXOS

"What a wonderful description of friendship among men—something seldom written about—and especially because [Epstein] dares to use the word 'love.' Normally that would take someone like me someplace other than pure friendship, but [the author insists] on using it as an important part of every real friendship. I'm from the northern part of Denmark where we seldom use expansive words like 'wonderful,' 'fantastic,' and 'love,' . . . even [when] talking about women. We find those words silly and exaggerated. Only Americans use these words.

"But through [this] book I have realized that friendship is like love: It has its ups and downs. Sometimes you wander into it without knowing it's a big mistake; it could be an attraction that then turns into repulsion (can you use that word in English?). So, I have learned a lot about love and friendship from this book. It has taught me that love is friendship and friendship is love and that I actually love several of my male friends. . . .

"They are also from the northern part of Denmark, and it wouldn't be appropriate in any way for me to tell them I love them. But I do. And [this] book has helped me to realize this. The friendship [Epstein writes] about includes zaniness. I couldn't survive any friendship and love without that."

—Lars Uggerhøj, PhD, Professor of Sociology and Social Work, Aalborg, Denmark

"In this modern world where closeness and support between men are still seen in some places as taboo, it's refreshing to come across a book like *Men as Friends*. Filled with true stories of male friendships, it peels away cultural layers of embarrassment that have historically hampered the love and respect that many men have for each other but are hesitant to express. Irwin Epstein's book shows the love, sadness, and the beauty in his exploration on this subject. A win-win on every level!"

—Mike "Chico" Randle, Lead Guitarist and Vocalist, LOVE-Revisited Band

Men As Friends:
From Cicero to Svevo to Cataldo

by Irwin Epstein

ISBN 978-1-64663-993-9

Published by

◤ köehlerbooks™

3705 Shore Drive
Virginia Beach, VA 23455
800-435-4811
www.koehlerbooks.com

MEN AS FRIENDS

From Cicero to Svevo to Cataldo

IRWIN EPSTEIN

VIRGINIA BEACH
CAPE CHARLES

For Fran

ITALO SVEVO
Triestine Jew
Italian language tutor to James Joyce
Prior to Joyce an unknown writer
Joyce's model for Leopold Bloom
My preferred kind of godfather

(1861-1928)

"Strange! I feel so young and at the same time so different from what I was in my youth! Could this be ripe old age?"

Italo Svevo – Umbertino.

JAMES JOYCE
(1881-1941)

"Absence, the highest form of presence."

James Joyce

Letter to Lucia Joyce 1935.

FOREWORD

by Allen Frances, M.D.

"Man is by nature a social animal; an individual who is unsocial naturally and not accidentally is either beneath our notice or more than human."
~ARISTOTLE

UNLIKE WITH FAMILY, we get to pick our friends. And that's a good thing because family relationships often turn sour. George Burns, one of our first great stand-ups, said it for many of us when he mused, "Happiness is having a large, loving, caring, close-knit family living in another city."

Though Covid has slowed the rate of American geographic mobility slightly, our society remains remarkably on the move. In 2021, 8.4 percent of Americans changed residences. That meant having to make new friends and having to work to keep up with the old ones. The greater social isolation that Covid requires of us adds to the challenge of sustaining old friendships and starting new ones.

Meanwhile, how well or poorly we make and choose our friends goes a long way in deciding how happy we are, our physical and mental health, even how long we live. Studies have shown that lonely seniors have dramatically higher rates of medical problems, dementia, and premature death. Seniors lacking friends die as early as those who've smoked fifteen cigarettes a day or were addicted to alcohol. So for most of us, being good at friendship is a crucial survival skill.

It is therefore no great surprise that mankind's first literary creation, the 4,500-year-old *Epic of Gilgamish,* is a straight-out bromance. Or that the Bible is replete with quotes and vivid descriptions of friendships, good and bad. Or that Hollywood turns out buddy movies at a pace that rivals romantic heterosexual love stories. We could not have survived as a species without friendship. And without it, we cannot survive as individuals. Friendship fills life with meaning; its absence makes life painfully dull and hollow.

Irwin Epstein has a special gift for friendship and for describing in exquisite detail its highs and lows. His wise and witty book will help you become a better friend; find, make, and keep better friends; and avoid the dangers of toxic friendships, epitomized by Joey Adams's line, "With friends like these who needs enemies?" Irwin's book is a lovely and loving read—mellow, perceptive, poetic, and sometimes as funny as standup comedy.

A PhD career sociologist and international social-work researcher, Irwin describes his colorful and diverse friendships without the cluttering of theory or advice. Though not written as a "how-to" book on friendship, for me there are some clear lessons to be drawn from his vivid tales of fulfilling and unfulfilling friendships with men. And while written explicitly about male friendships, I think it's safe to say they apply to *all* human friendships. They are:

1. Don't be afraid to love your friends and to be loved back by them.

2. It's not the number of friendships that counts—it's their depth and endurance.

3. Choose your friends, rather than just letting your friends choose you.

4. Be of generous spirit, listen empathically, have tolerance, and keep your sense of humor about them, and also about yourself.

5. Old friends are often the best friends—treasure them— they will be there when you need them most.

6. Be forgiving, but not overly forgiving.

7. Avoid high maintenance people—they are rarely worth the agro.

8. Don't be afraid to end or "cool down" friendships that cause more harm than good.

9. Don't let your work get in way of your friendships—either as a distraction, or a cause of disagreement, or because of rivalry.

10. Friendship is especially important, but especially vulnerable, late in life.

I'm pleased to say that Irwin and I are friends and have led in many ways parallel lives. Both of us survived a difficult parent, the streets of Brooklyn and Queens, and the rigors of child labor. Both of us found salvation in school, sports, books, movies, the beach—and friendships. We've both had the same kinds of great and not-so-great friends. And both of us had extremely lucky lives and have wonderful wives.

But there is one great difference between us. He has a gift that I completely lack—he remembers his life in such vivid detail while mine just flew by in an indistinct blur. However, recently he reminded me that memory can be a blessing as well as a curse. Fortunately for me, his friendship memories have greatly stimulated my own—and whether you are a man or a woman, young or old, gay or straight or anywhere on the constantly changing set of categories with which we identify, they will also stimulate yours.

While reading the book, you will doubtless feel the same urge I did to connect more often with current friends, to reconnect with some precious ones lost along the way, and to savor the memory of those who have passed. Lucky for us the internet now makes easier the first two, but our remaining brain cells and associations make available the third. This has given me the nudge to do all three. I hope it does the same for you.

Allen Frances, MD
Professor and Chair Emeritus
Department of Psychiatry & Behavioral Science
Duke University

Author of *Saving Normal: An Insider's Revolt Against Out-of-Control Psychiatric Diagnosis, DSM-5, Big Pharma, and the Medicalization of Ordinary Life.*

MARCUS TULLIUS CICERO
(106 BCE – 43 BCE)

*"Friendship improves happiness and abates misery,
by the doubling of our joy and
the dividing of our grief."*

———∞———

*"Friends, though absent,
are still present."*

———∞———

"Old age by nature is rather talkative."

From: *Treatises on Friendship and Old Age.*

D.H. LAWRENCE
(1885-1930)

"All my life I have wanted friendship with a man.
What is this sense?
Do I want friendliness?
I should like to see anybody being 'friendly' with me.
Intellectual equals?
Or rather equals in being non-intellectual...
Not something homosexual, surely?"

D.H. Lawrence

Quoted from "All my life I have wanted friendship with a man": Jeffrey Meyer, *Homosexuality and Literature, 1890-1930* (Athlone Press, 1977), p.134 referenced in *Burning Man: The Trials of D.H. Lawrence* by Frances Wilson, Farrar, Straus and Giroux, 2021.

THOMAS MANN
(1875-1955)

*"Solitude gives birth to the original in us, to beauty unfamiliar
and perilous – to poetry. But also,
it gives birth to the opposite:
to the perverse, the illicit, the absurd."*

Thomas Mann
Death in Venice.

BERNARD OLLIVIER
(1938-PRESENT)

"I brim with that kind of reckless optimism that compels people to verify information for themselves, whatever the cost...to push myself to my limits by the time I arrive at the end of this long and overdue voyage of self-discovery."

Walking to Samarkand
Bernard Ollivier, 2001 translated from the French by Dan Golembeski, 2020.

TABLE OF CONTENTS

INTRODUCTION

THIS BOOK IS about men I've loved and a few I didn't. At a time when so much is written about male toxicity, predation, destructive aggression, and pathology—epitomized to my great embarrassment by Jeffrey Epstein, who shared my surname but little else—I thought it might be the perfect time for me to explore my loving and lasting relationships with the men who were my fellow travelers. Nice men. Good men. Imperfect men. Men trying. Like me.

In so doing, I consider a few men I might have loved but didn't, despite long years of highly productive collaborative work together as researchers, academics, and co-authors, as well as men who shared personal details of lives we each led, in part, together. Arguably, I might have loved them, but something always stood in the way. Something I didn't articulate to myself, nor until recently ever really thought about.

As I write this book, I wonder what it was that stood in the way. But I'm hoping that by examining those relationships in comparison with men I so easily and lastingly loved, I might come to understand more about me and them and our not-so-loving friendships. When I was a sociologist and research professor, I might have called the effort a "comparative case study." For me now, it is so much more. It's an effort to make meaning of an essential, structural axis of my life.

This book is written for men, for women who love men, and for women who don't believe men are capable of intimacy with other men, or women, or anyone at all. Most importantly, it is written for men who, for whatever reasons, might resist and thereby deny themselves this form of intimacy with other men and resist naming it *love*.

Recently, my wife, Fran, called my attention to a two-column death notice in the *New York Times*. The author, a man of approximately my age, wrote touchingly of a tender and mutually supportive friendship that survived seven decades he had shared with a guy named Eddie. After reading it, my competitive male *agro* impulse was, "I hope this guy isn't writing a memoir about Eddie and him," until Fran pointed out that, notwithstanding the profound grief and quotidian details of their friendship since the age of fifteen, the word *love* never appears in the notice.

Months later, it was August of 2022. We were in the hospital once again. Fran, my hero who had courageously done battle with three different cancers over the course of three decades, was receiving yet another form of chemotherapy. Though I had been a research consultant at the same hospital for over two decades, that day I was merely arm candy. As Fran dosed off, I asked whether she had anything I could read?

She handed me a rolled-up copy of the latest *New Yorker*. In it was a review by a woman about two books on the topic of male toxicity—one book about contemporary man and the other beginning with Neanderthals. Months later, my daughter forwarded an article from the *New York Times* about men's incapacity to forge deep and lasting friendships with other men. Instructions were proffered, instructions my daughter pointed out were written by a woman. She wondered why?

It was time for *my* book, we both agreed. For all their concupiscence and cupidity, I thought both contemporary men and Neanderthals had gotten a bad rap. Nearing age eighty-five, I couldn't have been there caring for Fran so devotedly if not for the lifelong support and love of my various male friends.

This book is about them. It harkens to the distant voice of

Marcus Tullius Cicero, the Roman statesman who wrote about friendship and old age. It listens to the more recent Modernist voice of Italo Svevo, the Triestine Jew whose essays about aging echoed Cicero but added a tender, self-effacing humor. Svevo was arguably Joyce's model for Leopold Bloom in *Ulysses*. Joyce was famously quoted to say that men could not love other men. If I were a literary scholar, I might argue that Joyce loved Bloom and Svevo, by proxy.

But if I have any objective at all, it's to embark on a fearless journey of discovery, self-understanding, and self-healing like that of Bernard Ollivier's, but without my schlepping to Samarkand—savoring without privation a celebration of that part of my life that has been a joy and comfort by memorializing the not-famous men who made those emotions possible in good and in bad times. If my primary purpose seems selfish, at least it's well-intended. This is not a revenge memoir—about my father or about men I could not truly love. Though I am at times critical of their behaviors, I mean no ill to their memories. After all, he was my father, and they remained my friends.

CHAPTER 1

MY FATHER, MY PATERFAMILIAS*

"As a semantic term, paterfamilias thus connoted heads of household who were thought to combine the affective tenderness of a father with the stern coercion of a slave-owner in ordering their households."
~Wikipedia.

NOT EVERY PATERFAMILIAS is tender. A master diamond setter by trade, my father was paranoid, perceptive, and psychologically powerful by adult inclination. He wasn't born that way, but the external circumstances of his life shaped him. At work, those attributes came in handy.

Just as for all diamond setters—skilled artisans who set gemstones into fine jewelry—survival and success in business meant being obsessively attentive to minute details and having hands that could cease pushing platinum and white gold prongs over at precisely the right moment the valuable stone in the center of the engagement ring is as secure as the marriage it portends. But despite lofty promises, marriages dissolve, and despite their notorious strength, diamonds can chip and even explode with the slip of a tool. If you're setting someone else's 5-carat, perfect blue-white gem in a platinum engagement ring and you inadvertently break it, you eat it.

Genuine emeralds are much softer than diamonds and often internally flawed. Consequently, they are even easier to break, but just as scratchy going down the gullet. In my father's tiny workshop, when emeralds were being set, the radio was turned off. Conversation was unthinkable.

The atmosphere in my father's workplace alternated between one of extreme stress and occasional breaks for casual schmoozing with visiting Orthodox Jewish diamond dealers whose long black coats held wallets full of diamonds—each with its own stories of origin, ownership, polishing, travel, and consensually arrived-at value. Stories were told in English, with a smattering of Yiddish. When I was there, I was grateful for the English. The stories themselves were often ironic with a humorous ending. Like when the estate buyer next door gave his wife a recently acquired diamond pin to wear to a wedding—where the owner of the stolen pin and her husband, a judge, summoned the police! It was in the *New York Daily News*. Front page!

My father was a gifted storyteller as well, but all his stories started in danger and ended in near disaster. Like when he walked home from work in a hurricane and nearly stepped over a dead body that the police had not properly cordoned off. If my father hadn't been so alert, he could have been electrocuted as well just by touching the body.

His narrow, two-workbench office was at 71 Nassau Street in downtown Manhattan—a jewelry manufacturing district far from and lesser known than the infamous Diamond District on West 47th Street. Though in a jewelry-dedicated office building— now a luxury residential condominium—it was neither an office, a store, nor a lowly workshop to him. Instead, he referred to it as "the place." He did piecework, in which he charged by the individual necklace, ring, or brooch and paid in cash. Records— one for each customer—were kept in easily discarded brown pocket notebooks, should the IRS arrive unannounced.

I started working for him on Saturdays when I was about ten, and my not-so-comforting introduction to the neighborhood was his telling me that convicted criminals caught anywhere on the streets surrounding the place were *ipso facto* in violation of their paroles and subject to arrest by plainclothesmen (a.k.a. "flatfoots") who cruised the busy streets. I imagined streets full of criminals, but he assured me that I was safe because no one would suspect a kid like me was picking up and dropping off precious jewelry. But I was instructed to *always* (emphasis his) walk with one hand in the pocket holding valuables to thwart the many pickpockets lurking on the street just looking for an innocent and unsuspecting kid like me.

With proper training and nurturance, paranoia can flower at an early age. Fearing cops as well as thieves, I imagined being taken for a thief or pickpocket and having to answer to a very big and tough detective's, "Where'd you get the diamonds, kid?" Since my father thought that all cops were crooked as well, this set of contradictions troubled me greatly even when he just sent me to get him an extra-lean corned beef sandwich from the deli across the street. "Slip the counter man a quarter," he'd say, "*before* you order, so you'll be sure to get it the way I want it."

Upstairs in his workshop I felt no safer. The space tolerated only two side-by-side jeweler's workbenches—one for him and the other for a potential diamond-setter renter. But no one could tolerate my father's rants for longer than their thirty-day deposit.

I withstood it for years, as a gopher, a diamond-setting apprentice, and ultimately a Florentine engraver, which sounds more impressive than it was. But the money was good, there was no risk of breakage in what I did, and he paid me in cash.

In the space behind my father's back stood a behemoth of a combination safe in which unfinished jewelry and loose precious stones safely slept in the evening. During the day, however, the safe doors were intentionally left wide open in case an armed robbery occurred and my father needed to hide while reaching the phone to call the cops. As exciting as that sounded to me as a spectator for multiple reasons—like him getting shot by the cops or the robbers—that never happened. But I wondered, *What about me?* I would be left exposed.

Behind the safe was an electronic gate, which could be opened at the push of a button under his benchtop after visually identifying whoever had entered the outer office. Identification was accomplished via mirrors strategically placed on the right of his bench and the left of mine.

I had no such button, and leaving my seat, I could open the gate by hand. Nonetheless, I was instructed to never open the gate *even* to a recognized name or face without first determining whether they were alone. A gunman could always be lurking behind.

At home and at work, like many paranoid individuals, my father was exquisitely attentive to the phenomenology of the social slight and the potential for what is referred to in certain communities now as "disrespect." Plots against him and his family, risks by association, nefarious motives hidden within quotidian pleasantries—these were his psychological stock and trade.

A great American sociologist of deviant behavior, Edwin C. Lemert, demonstrated empirically that paranoiacs are quite correct in thinking that coworkers, relatives, and acquaintances *do* plot to avoid them and talk about them behind their backs— because of their paranoid behavior. My father was no exception.

Once crossed, whether innocently, intentionally, or criminally, he never forgot and never forgave. Early in my brother's marriage, in exchange for rent, he and my sister-in-law lived in our finished basement in Flushing Queens. Included in the rental was direct access to a free, non-coin-operated washer-dryer. A few weeks into their residency, my sister-in-law guilelessly overloaded our washing machine so severely that it warranted a call to a repairman. For the rest of his life and for this single infraction, she earned the sobriquet "S-Head" (a.k.a. "shithead") and was despised by him ever after. But the man never called her S-Head to her face though he would quite frequently to me. After all, she was still family.

Years later, at my father's funeral, a eulogizing rabbi was doing just fine with his computer-based questionnaire eulogy about someone he'd never met. The printout had blanks that I had filled in the night before with descriptive phrases like "child prodigy violinist," "forced to quit school and the violin to support his family at fourteen," "apprenticed as a diamond setter at sixteen," "sold only perfect blue-white diamonds" (not entirely true but that's what he claimed), and a "lifelong boxing fan."

Halfway through the eulogy the rabbi rested, paused dramatically, and said sonorously as only rabbis and borscht-belt comedians before the punchline can, "And the man never held a grudge." The rabbi was riffing. *I never wrote that!* My sister and I made a great effort to avoid each other's eyes. But when we could no longer, we exploded into laughter and coughing fits so loud that everyone in the chapel stared angrily at us through their handkerchiefs and real or pretend tears. Though we solemnly tried not to, we laughed spasmodically through the remainder of the service. And over the years, many times since.

One quality I did not write into the eulogy was my father's keen olfactory sense. I never thought of it as a positive trait because it was the cause of so much grief to me, my siblings, and my mother. His sense of smell could in the space of a moment transform an otherwise benign set of family meal circumstances into a frightening crisis.

Often, after work, he would come in the front door of our apartment and later our house for dinner, step inside, raise his left nostril suspiciously, and utter the words, "There's a foreign odor in this house." For us children it meant run for cover. For my mother it meant apologetically explaining that she was just trying a new recipe she thought he and the children might like. To which he would furiously stamp his foot and respond, "I want things to stay the way they are!"

When she did timorously branch out in the kitchen, she was careful always to make for him a full meal that she knew he would approve of and serve my brother, my sister, and me the experimental fare. Later in the meal, he might look over at what we were eating, take a forkful from one of our plates and on occasion ask my mother, "What's it called? Is there any left for me?" There always was. That could be one of her happiest moments in my poor mother's life. We could look up then.

Every Friday, for no reason other than alliteration, he became a *Marrano* Catholic for dinner and insisted on fish—more specifically fried flounder. The culinary/olfactory challenge this presented my mother was how to produce the flounder without the house smelling of frying fish. He hated that smell. Many an argument between my parents centered on this particular tautology.

Because he hated the smell of fresh paint as well, when our walls began to flake we moved to other apartments in other neighborhoods—partly to avoid the smell of the freshly painted apartment we had abandoned. Also, to improve our station in lower-middle-class life and to avoid the "boogies" moving into the neighborhood.

Consequently, we lived in a plethora of rented apartments, gradually moving from Brownsville to Crown Heights to East Flatbush. Mind you, that was long before Brooklyn was hip and happening. But each move still represented another rung up the ladder. It's hard to convey, however, what it was like moving from one cramped apartment to another, fueled by a menacing energy, with a force that wasn't about improvement so much as avoiding external enemies.

At home, my siblings and I were constantly monitored—not to protect, but to catch us out. Once caught, there were all manner of psychological and physical boundary violations, but the *dread* of what it might be was the worst. Constipation—real or imagined—was one enemy. Enemas were the only defense. The yelling and screaming would prickle my scalp, clench my anus, and take root in my gut as well as my psyche. For me and my sibs, it robbed us of the core thing all children need—a sense of unconditional love, safety, and security.

I entered life in 1938, in the New Lots section of Brooklyn, where mustachioed Italian old men still shepherded goats foraging for food on actual lots. The friendly clang of their bells came back to me decades later when my second wife and my daughter first traveled in Greece. I bought some goat bells in Athens and brought them home to Manhattan. Today they are of no use in New York City, certainly not in Brooklyn.

At four, I had my first girlfriend—Lucy. The ill-fated but memorable relationship lasted about an hour. One day, I was sitting on our stoop on Berriman Street, when a soulful, brown-eyed, and slight little girl approached me in a silvery green dress, told me her name, asked me mine, and then asked if I wanted to "play tea." I asked what that was. She said that she had a new tea set at home and if I wanted, I could come to her house and she would show me. I was immediately smitten and accompanied her to a basement apartment in a building next door where I now assume her father was the live-in superintendent (a.k.a. "super").

She ushered me into a darkly lit room with a dining table in the center. Many years later, visiting the Van Gogh Museum in Amsterdam, seeing "The Potato Eaters" immediately brought the scene back to me. Sitting on the smooth concrete floor, Lucy took out a green plastic tea set with cups, saucers, a pink tea pot, and dishes for imaginary cakes. After filling the teapot with water from the kitchen sink, she poured "tea" into each of our cups and set them on a pretend table on the floor for just the two of us. I don't remember what we talked about, but I remember our commenting about how delicious the tea and cakes were. We wiped our mouths with our hands after each sip and two-fingers full.

After a while her mother came in from the kitchen with an enormous mound of spaghetti in tomato sauce on an oval tray that she set in the middle of the not-pretend table with the same care with which Lucy placed our tea service. I'd had spaghetti before from a can and liked it, but I'd never seen so much on a single plate. The room smelled sweet and warm and comforting. I've loved cooking and eating pasta ever since.

Then Lucy's father came in, sat at the table wearing a tweed cap and a giant twirled-at-the-ends mustache, and began eating, slouched over the table. Next to his dish was a simple jam jar of dark red liquid. It looked like grape juice. I recognized the glass from ones we had at home, but not its contents. Now I know; red wine, probably chianti. He glanced at Lucy and me and smiled gently, not saying a word.

Then maybe a half-hour later, in an alto voice I still can hear, Lucy's mother told us to pack up the tea set, my parents might be worried about me. I headed back across the street, my heart full of Lucy.

Worried isn't the word. My mother stood on our steps crying hysterically. My father was enraged saying that he thought I'd been kidnapped and was about to call the police. While I understood their alarm at my disappearance, there was no affective tenderness displayed—or even relief. Just rage and hysteria.

On our front steps, my father grilled me about where I'd been. When I told him and about Lucy's tea set, both he and my mother went ballistic. "Did you drink the water? Those people are dirty. They're not Jewish. I could have her father fired and evicted and her mother arrested for letting you stay. Don't ever go there or talk to that girl again!"

An obedient child, I never did. At the time, I didn't understand. They had seemed so kindly and the room that they shared was loving and tension free. The scenario stayed with me, though I don't remember ever seeing Lucy again. I imagine her looking today like my daughter, Becs, who is part Italian on her mother's side.

My father's concerns about drinking water safety extended from family members to household pets. When we lived on Berriman Street, his father, my Grandpa Epstein, had a little dry-cleaning and pressing shop around the corner. Around the corner from that, he lived in a walk-up apartment above a synagogue with my agoraphobic Grandma Epstein who spent her days in a nightgown primping in front of a mirror. I don't think she ever said a word to me. She simply cried tenderly every time she saw me. My grandfather would begin each day by making a pot of chicken noodle soup, which would serve as both their lunch and dinner.

At his tailor shop, one wall was covered with yellow canaries in cages. They would sing through the day and especially on Sunday mornings at ten when the Hartz Mountain birdseed company had an orchestra play music on the radio for their canaries and his canaries to sing by. It was delightful and possibly also attributed to the revelation, years later, that the Hartz Mountain special canary mix contained cannabis seeds.

On Sunday mornings, Grandpa didn't work. While his canaries sang their hearts out, he played pinochle with his cronies drinking slivovitz (prune whisky) seated around the pressing machine, using its long pad as a makeshift card table. I loved the way they slammed their cards on the pad at the completion of a hand. And I loved the way my grandfather smacked the last drop of his schnapps on his palm then rubbed it on his face like aftershave, even when he didn't shave.

Like his son, my grandfather was an explosive man, who, despite the prohibition against Jews, fought for the Russians in the Russo-Japanese War. Once he came to this country, he worked for the International Garment Workers Union (ILGWU) as a goon roughing up strikebreakers who crossed picket lines. Once the union was officially recognized however, they set him loose. From then on, he was embittered that he wasn't rewarded with a cushy office job for his devotion to the labor movement. Instead, he went from "first one out to last back in" to no job at all because of his notorious temper. Feeling betrayed by the labor movement, with the little money he saved, he opened his small dry-cleaning and tailoring shop in the East New York section of Brooklyn.

At the store, pity the poor rabbi who came by asking for money for trees in Israel. Grandpa's anger trampled all religious and political causes. My father inherited his distrust and for this reason cautioned us never to even register as Republican or Democrat. "You never know when all the Democrats or all the Republicans will be rounded up and placed in concentration camps." The prescience of the paranoid?

More tenderly, Grandpa was always enthusiastically gifting us with items left in pockets and eagerly copped clothes left over thirty days. There was the hand-lettered sign to that effect above the counter, after all. His hand-me-downs never fit anyone in our family, though he insisted that with some slight alterations they would. They didn't, but I wish I had some of the abandoned ties today. As I recall, they were quite remarkable. And by then, they had been cleaned and pressed.

His *finding* things extended beyond the perimeter of the

store as well. One time he chased away a bunch of kids who were playing ball in the street and *found* a pretty neat baseball mitt for me and a bat for my brother.

Another time he showed up at our house unannounced with a stray dog. Frail and frightened, it is clear to me now that the dog had been severely abused. For reasons of his or her appearance (I didn't know which), I named the dog Whitey. Whitey and I quickly bonded. A few days later, Whitey was seen by my father drinking from our toilet bowl. My father was so repulsed that the next day I was informed that Whitey "ran away."

Later I learned that the dog had been driven gangster-style to Canarsie somewhere, a part of Brooklyn far from our home, and dumped there unceremoniously. Two days later, while I was still wondering why Whitey would run away, there was a scratching at our door.

Though my father expressed genuine amazement and admiration at Whitey's intelligence, cunning, and geographical sense, the next day Jimmy Hoffa had a pet in the New Jersey Meadowlands.

I both deeply loved and deeply feared my father. The love part must have been mostly instinctual, though in rare moments he could be loving, what Skinnerians would call *intermittent reinforcement*, the subtle combination of reward and punishment that leads victims to love their victimizers. At age eighty-five, I still remember his underarm smell when I haven't showered. I find it pleasing rather than offensive. I shower anyway. Regularly.

When I was about five, maybe a year after the tea party incident, my father told me that his worst fear for me was that I might grow up to become a "homo." A doctor, yes—a homo, no. A homo doctor, impossible. They don't exist. A doctor treating homos, revolting.

He claimed, and I think honestly believed, that this

acknowledgement of concern was for my own benefit and protection. In his view, homos were made by either proximity to other homos or by the seduction of innocents, like me. Either way, homos weren't born that way. They learned to "like it" from other homos. That's why they preferred one another's company, walked and talked that way. Much later in life as a sociology student, I learned that correlation and causation were not the same thing.

But as a child, I had neither capacity nor the authority to question his beliefs. When my PhD in sociology and my lived experience equipped me to challenge his unchangeable beliefs, I had no desire or inclination to weigh in on these epistemological questions. But as a developing child, my worry and confusion about my own sexual drives, inclinations, and desires were palpable. They began very early—with proximity to my father.

* * *

One day when I was also about five, my mother observed me rubbing my genitals against the corner of my mattress—a practice that she quickly stopped by telling me, "You might hurt yourself very badly by doing that." A bright lad, I pondered, *How could anything that felt so good be so bad?* But I sensed somehow that I couldn't say that. Asking why it was so harmful, she said my father would explain it all to me when he got home from work. *Oh Jesus!*

Sadly, for me, my siblings, and more children than all the sociologists in the world can count, the day's most hazardous time is "when daddy gets home." Heavily calloused from his work, my father was proud of his hard hands. Declaring total victory over his own children's potential for misbehavior, he was proud to tell relatives, neighbors, and friends that he only had to hit each of us once. Once he did, we remembered. That was true for me, I don't know about the others. But in our minds, the threat was always there.

After being told what my mother had witnessed me doing earlier in the day, an ominous silence fell over dinner. I was so scared. To my relief and astonishment, he was remarkably calm after dinner and neither yelled nor spanked me.

Instead, we had our first extended father-son talk about sex and the possibility of my becoming "queer." For no additional price, he threw in a lecture on the risk of contracting VD on public toilets and how I might transfer it to my undeserving mother via our own homely toilet seat. And there was also the threat of *"shiksas,"* who "by the way do have better legs," tricking me into getting them pregnant before I completed medical school. But at five, I hadn't even applied.

Looking from side to side to see whether my mother (who, by the way, didn't have great legs) was listening, he cryptically cautioned me to always remember, "If you use your pencil, be sure to use a rubber eraser." It wasn't until I was in my twenties that I understood the pencil metaphor. I laughed to myself out loud when it occurred to me but didn't bother to explain why to my girlfriend in the moment.

His entire sex lecture probably took an hour, but felt like a year. My head was spinning with things I didn't understand and couldn't ask. My unnatural attraction to my mattress now effectively extinguished, I did not grow up to open a successful Mattress Firm franchise. This is not a rags-to-riches memoir. It is a *survival* memoir of sorts, but not an existential one.

What I think was the secret of my relative success at becoming a reasonably well-functioning human being was an innate and inexplicable sense that something in my family portrait was very wrong. From as early as I can remember, I knew that I was living in a madhouse in both senses of the word, and that if I could survive until adulthood, I would be fine. I have no idea how I knew that, but I did. I had few models, no mentors, only my very sensitive and intelligent mother, who was also a slave to my father's vagaries. She excused them by saying while he was alive, "he means well," and when he was gone, "he meant well." But I'm still not entirely sure he did.

In my teens, he still openly expressed the worry that I was a "homo," "queer," "fag," "fairy," or "swish," questioning my cultural interests in music, art, and literature and my associations with male friends that he might judge effeminate.

To readers suspecting his homophobia belied a closeted case of protesting too much, I'll throw a few juicy scraps. In what psychologists might refer to as my *untroubled latency years,* every week he and I watched the Friday Night Fights together on our first black-and-white TV.

He loved watching Blacks beat the hell out of each other. I use that term descriptively, he called them "schvartzers" derisively. Even better, he liked watching Whites, like the famed Jake LaMotta, beating the hell out of Blacks. But without the slightest hesitation, whether Black or White, he would comment admiringly about particular boxer's "perfect Y formation"—wide shoulders and narrow waists and above all, their muscularity. And though he was a total racist, he particularly praised Black male physiques.

When I was fourteen and my mother was forty, she became pregnant. With the announcement, as though immensely proud of his achievement, he told my eighteen-year-old brother Marty and me that pregnancy at my mother's age was extremely dangerous and misbehavior on our part could kill both her and the baby, all the while bragging to others that he "gave her a baby because she was bored and had nothing to do at home."

As we always did, my brother and I behaved. We were too scared not to. When my mother went into labor, Marty was given money to pay for our first restaurant meal alone. At first, my brother and I were thrilled that we could order anything we wanted, but once the food arrived, I could barely eat—never a problem for Marty, who was six feet to my less than five. Still, we were both enormously relieved when mother and baby survived. And we now had a baby sister, Carole.

My brother and I both doted on the new baby, but I was enlisted in caring for her during what I now understand to be my mother's severe post-partum depression. Marty was in Junior Achievement after school at the time strenuously working his way towards "most likely to succeed."

Expecting only exaltation and adulation for his gift to her, my father had no explanation for my mother's unexpected depression. Mostly he was angry. Consequently, in my first year of high school I had my first baby to take care of.

To my amazement and to my parents' rescue, I discovered that I loved taking care of a baby and became a live-in babysitter/ *au pair* and benign father figure to Carole until I moved out when she was about six. Though I loved loving her, I was enormously confused about my gender, my role in the family, and my image of myself at school. But I kept things going at home until my mother gradually emerged from her depression.

At the time we were already living in Queens. After a fifteen-year apartment rental tour of Brooklyn fleeing the housepainters and the equally threatening incoming Blacks, my parents bought a newly built, one-family house in Flushing, Queens.

While I was in Flushing High School and he was in DeWitt Clinton High School in the Bronx, I met Jerry, a boy who became a man that I have loved for nearly seventy years without interruption—longer than any of my marriages and recently reconfirmed via phone. We never had sex together or wanted

to—*not that there would have been anything wrong if we did*
(emphasis Jerry Seinfeld's).

———————◇◇———————

At the time I met him, Jerry lived in the Bronx but visited
his Aunt Vera and Uncle Frank and three girl cousins just up
the street from our Flushing home on weekends. From a large,
extended, Italian American, working-class family, I knew
him only as "Jerry-from-the-Bronx" for more than a year. We
played stickball every weekend together with a couple of other
locals in our wide and newly paved street. What a treat that
was in comparison to the narrow and busy streets I'd known
in Brooklyn, which only allowed for "hit the penny" on the
sidewalk, "Chinese handball," allowing one bounce against the
building wall, or "stoopball," but with many interruptions for
oncoming and horn-honking cars.

In stickball, Jerry could hit a pink Spalding (a.k.a. "Spaldeen")
rubber ball with a sawed-off broomstick the proverbial "two
sewers." A "sewer" is the distance between manhole covers. In
stickball jargon that was the bar that everyone wanted to surpass.

In high school Jerry was a gymnast. My father described him
admiringly to Jerry's father with a hint of salivation at each corner
of his mouth as having "a body like a Greek God." Though I might
have worried about my father's attraction to Jerry, my father never
worried about Jerry and me. After all, Jerry dated cheerleaders.

What my father didn't know, and I learned only recently,
was when Jerry-from-the-Bronx was in the Bronx and not on
the parallel bars in the gym, his life was like that of a young
Robert DeNiro in a Martin Scorsese film—hanging around with
and engaging in illegal activities with young Mafia wannabees.
For Jerry, it turned out, Flushing meant freedom from having
to stay on the right side of local gang members and engaging

in dangerous activities that increasingly frightened as they escalated. Now, he's a very successful clinical psychologist. He could have been a Soprano. Or a filmmaker.

Fortunately for Jerry and ultimately for me, his parents relocated to Flushing to be closer to Aunt Vera and Uncle Frank. That meant he lived a couple of blocks from me. That really set the stage for the growing intimacy of our friendship while we were each living at home and going to different New York colleges, his public and mine private. Jerry went to CCNY, and I went to NYU.

However, unlike the pass I got with Jerry, my budding friendship with my new NYU pal, Don, drove my father batshit. Don read French novels, knew lyrics from Broadway musicals, and loved Gene Kelly movies. And he wasn't ashamed to say so. Don would unhappily agree that many people, including his own father, thought his gestures effeminate. But as far as I knew, despite his suspect mannerisms, he seemed quite confident about his heterosexuality and his attractiveness to women. In fact, we competed for the attentions of the same girls. Because of my lack of confidence, I always deferred to him in that competitive arena.

Over breakfast one morning, my father confided about having had a terrible nightmare in which Don and I were taking off somewhere together in a taxi. Seeing this in his dream, my father reached through the open window of the taxi to try to *rescue* me, but I refused to be rescued. He found it very disturbing and wondered what it meant.

That summer Don and I did run away together to work at a camp for disabled children and adults in upstate New York. My father was not happy.

———————◦∞◦———————

Conditions at Camp Jen-Ed were hard. Some children had

full leg braces, some were blind, others deaf, and others with severe cerebral palsy were in wheelchairs. Despite its outward appearance as a noble and eleemosynary effort to provide a much-needed vacation for children who had been cooped up all winter, and for parents who desperately needed a break, it was a Dickensian business. We had hot water only on parents' visiting day. Towards the end of the summer, simple medical supplies like aspirin and Band-Aids ran out, and counselors were encouraged to replenish them with our own money for the campers. The food was abominable. Counselors were told that they would be fired on the spot if they ever entered the kitchen where the ominous "Chef Louie" commanded a staff of derelicts.

Campers were told to be absolutely sure to let Louie know a day before their birthday so he could make them a birthday cake. Towards the end of summer when kitchen supplies must have been running low, one of the boys in my bunk had his birthday celebrated with a seeded rye bread covered with shocking pink strawberry icing. The kids ate it anyway. I only watched.

One Sunday in August my parents decided to visit. My father probably thought I was trysting with Don and wanted to affect another rescue. *In his dreams!* I had a very sweet, deaf, *shiksa* girlfriend named Alice who waited tables at the camp, but introducing her to my parents would create another kind of nightmare for us all. Anyway, I was happy because I knew their car would be loaded with my mother's cooking.

What I didn't count on was the car. Hearing it approach on the gravel path to my bunk, I looked up to discover the Buick newly repainted fire-engine red and ambulance white as a gift for me and a "chick-magnet" for attracting girls when I returned home in the fall—a flashy "cat car" that young girls couldn't resist.

To his utter dismay and disappointment, I secured my driver's license and used the car mainly to drive to an outpatient mental health clinic at Hillside Hospital for psychotherapy.

Even there, where psychopathology was the official currency, his paranoia represented a major obstacle. Hillside offered a sliding scale payment arrangement for psychotherapy. However, since I was under twenty-one, I needed parental permission to receive therapy and IRS tax information was required.

Much of my father's work income involved undeclared cash payments. So, he theorized that anyone in his right mind at Hillside would wonder how someone with my father's reported income could afford to drive such a flashy car to get there. This contradiction would both raise Hillside's fee and, worst of all, trigger a call to the IRS from which Hillside would reap a 10 percent bounty for reporting his underreported income. And why did I need psychotherapy anyway with a car like that? Plus, "psychotherapy is bullshit" and I might have blamed him for all my made-up problems.

To feel so close to help and have it yanked from reach tipped me over the edge, and I made one half-hearted and one strategic attempt at suicide. Fear of losing me spurred my mother to override him this one time. I was so grateful, though he of course felt betrayed by us both. The good news was Hillside waved the fee and he wasn't audited.

A parallel and arguably less extreme issue came up regarding my college career. I was an excellent student in high school, studying and loving Latin in preparation for medical school. I was offered no choice, however, about going to a college away from home because my brother—always a mediocre student but an aspiring businessman—had gone away to a private, business-oriented Fenn College in Cleveland. Availing himself of all manner of extra-curricular activities—fraternity, sailing club, debate team—he barely made it through his first year.

As a result, my father pulled the financial plug on him but extrapolated the prohibition about going away to college to me. No way was I going to exploit his hard-earned income to have a good time at his expense. I had to choose a commuter college and live at home. Period!

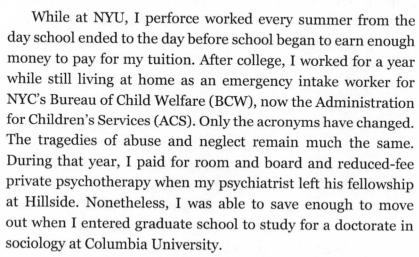

While at NYU, I perforce worked every summer from the day school ended to the day before school began to earn enough money to pay for my tuition. After college, I worked for a year while still living at home as an emergency intake worker for NYC's Bureau of Child Welfare (BCW), now the Administration for Children's Services (ACS). Only the acronyms have changed. The tragedies of abuse and neglect remain much the same. During that year, I paid for room and board and reduced-fee private psychotherapy when my psychiatrist left his fellowship at Hillside. Nonetheless, I was able to save enough to move out when I entered graduate school to study for a doctorate in sociology at Columbia University.

Ironically, the event that precipitated my moving out and on involved a physical confrontation with my father over a dog he'd bought allegedly as a pet for Carole. She'd named the dog "Blackie" for obvious reasons. My father, who always claimed to love dogs, was really in love with obedience. What he wanted most in a dog was neither loyalty nor unconditional affection like normal people. He wanted a dog that would play when he wanted to play and tease but never snap at him no matter how provocative he was. A dog that would never relieve itself in the wrong place and always drink from the right place. Unfortunately, his skills at obedience training were as twisted as his sex-education skills.

One Saturday night, I returned home about two in the morning from a first date feeling quite pleased with myself for reasons I won't enumerate. Thinking I would just get to bed and replay events that had taken place after a movie and coffee at Rienzi's in Greenwich Village, I was greeted instead by yet another primal-scream-worthy scene.

Blackie had peed on the kitchen floor. My father was in his boxer shorts and stockinged feet with a rolled up *Daily News* in his hand chasing Blackie around the kitchen trying to beat a confession from the poor dog. Thinking of my sister's innocent love for the puppy (and no doubt triggering my own loss of Whitey), I became so enraged that I grabbed the newspaper from his hand and threw him to the kitchen floor.

He was quite a bit heavier and stronger than I was at the time. Neither of us could believe what had just happened. After a very pregnant silence, he scrambled to his feet and while returning to his and my mother's bedroom, said, "I want you out of this house!" and slammed the door.

Shortly after that incident I attended a student orientation meeting in the Graduate Sociology Department at Columbia, where Arnie and I discovered that we both took the No. 7 train home. We found a place to share in Manhattan a few days later.

When I moved out my father said he didn't understand why.

———◦◦◦———

How I survived my childhood is explained better than I can in psychoanalyst Alice Miller's book *The Drama of the Gifted Child,* originally published in German in 1979, then translated as *Prisoners of Childhood* by Basic Books in 1981, and later republished under its current title, with the subtitle *The Search for the True Self.*

Unfortunately, I read this revelatory book much later in life than I needed to but fortunately when I was already a father. In the Amazon online product description, Miller is quoted as saying:

"When I used the word 'gifted' in the title, I had in mind

neither children who received high grades in school nor children talented in a special way. I simply meant all of us who have survived an abusive childhood thanks to an ability to adapt even to unspeakable cruelty by becoming numb. . . . this 'gift' [my emphasis] offered us by nature, we would not have survived."

But Miller goes on to say that survival is not enough. Something else must follow.

As a legacy for which I am grateful, my father's meticulous paranoia left me with some inherently neutral traits that I somehow transformed into positive social skills, like telling jokes at no one's expense but mine. And a love of storytelling.

He also left me with an enjoyment and mastery of phenomenology as a sociologist rather than as an angry sociopath. An appreciation of the power of metaphor. A slavish attraction (if not addiction) to alliteration, which is adumbrated shamelessly in this chapter. An aesthetic sensibility from the details of plating food to helping Fran match a scarf to her outfit, to apartment renovation and architectural design. A leg man who feels preternaturally attracted to slender women with wide shoulders. It's just the way I am.

As a single father, whenever I got angry, I had to stop myself countless times to inhibit my most destructive impulses, which surfaced all too easily. In their place I tried to substitute other more loving, tender, and empathic responses. Yes, I did dump a bowl of pasta on my complaining four-year-old son Daniel's head once, but we both laughed as the strings of spaghetti slid down his surprised cheeks. At fifty-six, his continued and unbridled love for pasta and expressed love for me cannot possibly be a reaction formation.

Evolutionary biologists use the term *survivals* to refer to parts of the human body that once served a function but no longer do. The vermiform appendix is the most frequent example given. In humans it serves no positive function at all but can cause serious trouble. With the help of several therapists, dear friends, and a fulfilling career as a teacher, researcher, and academic writer, I have been able to find, as Miller would say, my *true self*—capable of loving men as well as women. The remainder of this book is my first attempt to articulate to myself and others how and with whom.

CHAPTER 2

JERRY...THEN

Y OU ALREADY KNOW how Jerry and I met. It was the '50s and McCarthyism dominated the headlines. I'd just discovered Alan Freed's late-night R&B broadcasts from Cleveland and secretly enjoyed unbridled emotional freedom and uninhibited joy in our finished basement at two in the morning.

Jerry and I were both in our teens then—he a few years younger than I. As mentioned, our friendship took root over stickball but blossomed when "Jerry-from-the Bronx" became "Jerry-from-Flushing, Queens." Better yet, two blocks away. To Jerry's parents, Sam and Mickey, Jerry was precious. An only child and the only son in an extended Italian family of many girls, he was doted over and catered to by his parents. Especially his mother.

His father, Sam, was a quiet man who ran the meat department at a high-end Gristede's in Manhattan. Though taciturn at home, it's quite possible that Sam came to life from behind the counter, dealing with the maids of the rich, who were buying for their bosses but copping a few cutlets on the side to take home to their families. Sam slipped them into the monthly bills of their bosses, a carnivore's form of stealing from the rich and giving to the poor. Still Sam, silent or garrulous Sam, was remembered every Christmas by his privileged clientele with a cash gift for the quality and meticulousness of his butchering. A portion of the gift might then be shared with the maids who purchased the meats. Behind the counter, whatever his persona, Sam was king.

At home however, Mickey ruled the roost. A charmingly sharp-tongued and critically observant woman, I still remember her glowing olive complexion and smiling light blue eyes from whenever I visited. But in truth, she only had eyes for Jerry. Jerry was her prince.

And she strove to meet his needs. His needs were her requirements. For example, Jerry liked his button-down shirts open at the collar, but not too open. So, Mickey lovingly sewed snaps on all his shirts between the collars and first buttons. I vaguely recall something about his not liking it when his socks slipped down to his ankles. So, Mickey reinforced the elastics. Nothing, I mean nothing, was too good for her Jerry. Of course, she was a great cook as well, but everything had to be just as Jerry liked it. Lemon, not vinegar on his salad. Rigatoni with lines. "Sunday Gravy" with meatballs on a separate platter from the already meticulously sauced rigatoni. But Jerry had to grate the cheese himself. Rigatoni pushed aside on his plate to accommodate the meatball and porkchop, but never on top. Nothing touching. Nothing messy. Everything neat.

Jerry's Uncle Frank and Aunt Vera and their three daughters—Linda, Susan, and Donna—lived just up the block from us. Vera was a coquettish, playfully attractive, and understanding woman whom Jerry adored. I remember her as always laughing at people's foibles but never critical of people's imperfections as Mickey was. To Vera, Jerry was the perfect nephew and to Mickey the perfect son, though probably for very different reasons. Vera was accepting. Mickey was exacting.

Jerry was always a man's man. A tall, handsome, zit-free De Niro type and a superb athlete, he majored in mechanical engineering at City College—a public college where working class and lower-middle-income students climbed their way out of poverty. Also, a commuter college, to which he came and went via bus and subway like I did. The only difference was the subway route and the cost of tuition, which was my albatross.

By no means does this imply that Jerry didn't hustle for money. Winters, he sought night work with the NYC Department of Sanitation doing snow removal. Jewish boys didn't do that. Italian boys did. But even there, Jerry just naturally found himself among the snow-removal elite. He didn't shovel snow. Instead, his job was to ride in the passenger seat of garbage trucks, informing drivers when they came too close to parked cars with their plows.

These all-nighters also turned out to be quite lucrative as well as enjoyable for Jerry and the drivers. When not cleaning the city streets they would be clearing the non-municipal parking lots of bowling alleys and supermarkets and finishing up at diners where trenchermen-sized four-in-the-morning breakfasts were, of course, on the house. These little side jobs were where the cash money was really made. For the rest, Jerry would get a check from the city, months later.

To me, Jerry lived a charmed life, but it didn't always feel like that to him. As an only child and an only son among a swarm of girl-cousins, his parents' and his relatives' expectations of him were high and exacting. Finish college, get a good, secure, white-collar job that pays well and doesn't require working with your hands, like Sam-the-meat-cutter or equally silent Uncle Frank, an iron monger who made fences and guard rails. Frank's hands were immense and splayed from his work. Sam's were jumbo, too, just not so large as Frank's.

Both Jerry and I were expected to work during the summers. As a mechanical engineering student his summer jobs were as a draftsman. And he was very good at it. After canvassing thirty engineering firms by mail, he received one positive response, and each successive summer improved his position based on the past summer's performance. His family thought for sure he would become a mechanical engineer. They would have been quite happy with that outcome.

Though graduating from college with an engineering degree, in his senior year of college he switched majors to psychology, realizing that the job market was flooded with mechanical engineers who were working alongside him as draftsmen in his summer jobs. Coincidentally, my first summer jobs were with a national electrical energy firm that my brother had worked for in previous summers. Instead of doing drafting, my work involved filing the drawings of draftsmen and draftswomen and hand-printing minutely lettered inventories of new equipment installed in electrical power plants in Midwestern cities I'd never heard of. To earn extra money, I often worked twelve-hour days and came home barely able to see.

My happiest times during college were spent with Jerry and his extended family. He then lived in an apartment just a walk away where I would escape my all-too-nuclear family to spend time with Jerry talking about all manner of things and making multi-layered sandwiches with perfectly sliced and packaged cold cuts that his father brought home from work. Every slice of roast beef or Black Forest ham or prosciutto or capicola, Swiss or Munster cheese, had a tissue separating it from the next slice of whatever it was. For lunches we would pile various combinations in various orders according to the mandates of deli-science and our tastes of the day. These required much mandibular stretching to consume, but between bites and swallows we talked in depth about our feelings, our families, our male friends, school, and principally about girls.

Though I don't think Jerry was as oppressed by his family as me, Mickey was problematic to Jerry as well as to his father, Sam, for whom Jerry felt sorry. Opinionated and sharp-eyed, you always knew what Mickey thought, and it was often cast in caustic and critical comments. Her scrupulous attention to Jerry's needs could be a double-edged sword for him, but her pasta made everything right for both of us. And a deep-dish apple pie she made with heavy cream in a square baking dish was something to dream about.

Summers were the best when I would be invited to go to the beach with Jerry and his extended family. Two cars would leave very early Saturday morning from Flushing to "Joneses" Beach to snag parking spots close to the beach and a charcoal grill near the parking lot for long rings of Sam's handmade pork sausage and other meats. Mickey and Vera would make all kinds of salads and there would be an immense cooler of beer for the men and soda for the ladies and kids. But the best of the best were Mickey's eggplant "sangwiches," which would start out cold but warm to greasy perfection in the sun when liberated from carefully arranged icepacks.

Once at the wide beach, Jerry and I would leave the men and women behind to get the fire going and the food and drinks together. The little kids played in the sand. The teenage girls mooned around cultivating their tans. We weren't interested. Our eyes were only for the morning tide of the dark green and bracingly cool Atlantic waves. We were there above all to bodysurf and eat.

For me it was ecstatically liberating to ride and survive powerful natural forces and laugh when we emerged, the way I never could laugh at home. Even when we were knocked over. For Jerry, it might have been simply gymnastically fun. We never talked about what it meant for us other than to remark about the height of the wave and how far into shore we were able to ride it.

When we were thoroughly exhausted, we'd find our parallel towels and lie prone with our backs to the ocean, the better to spot attractive girls on the beach.

"Well, what about that one with the black hair, she's really pretty?"

"No, I think the blond on the blanket next to her is not as pretty, but what a great body!" Or words to that effect.

The closest Jerry and I ever came to sex together was at Jones Beach one summer. Don't be thinking scenes of Deborah Kerr and Burt Lancaster in *From Here to Eternity* or alternatively of Lancaster and Montgomery Clift with Jerry and me locked in embrace rolling in the surf together. Instead, the scene was a young couple making out on a blanket within eyeshot of our strategic positions. We were thoroughly enjoying their cavorting and laughing with each other, until the lovers were obviously overcome by their passions. "Holy shit!" With total disregard for anyone else on the beach, let alone Jerry and me eagerly watching, they suddenly pulled their blanket over them and began screwing for real—quite obviously, vigorously, audibly, and at length while Jerry and I became speechless.

And that's when Mickey started calling across the wide expanse of beach to tell us that lunch was ready. Pinned to the sand by our uncontrollable and recalcitrant teenage erections barely covered by our matching black Speedos, Jerry and I could not spring to her attention the way pleasure-seeking organs sprang to ours. On normal occasions we would eagerly race to the picnic area. This was indeed a special occasion. Unaccustomed to not seeing us show up immediately, she kept calling louder and louder sounding alternatively more panicked and exasperated.

Now it was more like a scene from a Fellini film, Jerry and I hobbling forward on the blazing-hot noontime sand slowly enough for our erections to subside but fast enough for Mickey to stop shouting and to keep the soles of our feet from burning. The film's musical accompaniment could have been de Falla's

"Ritual Fire Dance."

After feebly trying to explain what took us so long, the warmed-by-the sun, unctuous eggplant sangwiches were all the more delicious with our icy-cold sodas—the cans cooling the soles of our feet between slurps.

We laughed much of the way home, and to this day I can never screw an umbrella into the sand without fondly thinking about that amorous day at the beach with Jerry.

I felt so comfortable and welcome at Vera and Frank's just three houses away from my own that I even brought a date to a New Year's party there. Jerry's family welcomed her warmly and casually as just another guest. They had no idea what that meant to me. Just down the street I hoped my parents wouldn't see us so I wouldn't face the interrogation that would inevitably follow about Deena's religion, what her parents did . . . etc.

Several years later, that's where I brought my future wife. She was Italian American and daughter of a dean, and after my own parents had said she'd make my now deceased Grandpa Epstein "roll over in his grave," I took her three doors down to my second family. At Vera and Frank's on Christmas Eve, I happily shared a Feast of the Seven Fishes and ate linguini and white clam sauce for the first time.

Jerry's switch to psychology caused as much consternation in his family as my not going to medical school did in mine. While I was working at a summer camp for orthopedically disabled children, Jerry was thinking of a career as a prosthetist, using his knowledge of physics to design prosthetics. Though we were casting about in different career directions we both wanted to help people—whatever that meant. My thought was to enter social work, using my understanding of sociology to ameliorate social problems. For reasons still unclear, neither of us wanted to become what we thought of as *real* doctors. Perhaps that was our only form of rebellion we imagined available to us. Two good boys. In the range of possibilities, it was admittedly pretty lame. But his parents had no idea what clinical psychologists did for a living. Likewise, my parents had no idea what sociologists did. But sociologist was perfect for me, and clinical psychologist was perfect for Jerry.

After we each married, Jerry completed his PhD at Duke, and I completed mine at Columbia. We had academic careers teaching at public universities and consulting in our respective applied fields—helping people, or at least trying. We both had a son and then a daughter.

As a consequence of my divorce seven years later, and though it was officially called joint custody, I became a single father for several years, raising my children until, unexpectedly, they rejoined their mother, Lyn, in their teens in Chicago, when Kayla and I married in Michigan and relocated to New York in 1979.

Tragically, Jerry's wife and high school sweetheart, Christine, died of cancer in 1985 at forty, leaving him with two young children to raise completely on his own. I can still hear Jerry's howl of grief on a late-night telephone phone call telling me that Christine had died. That was also the year of my second divorce.

Jerry sustained himself through the years that immediately followed her loss raising his kids, excelling in his academic career at the State University of New York (Buffalo), and designing and commissioning a playground in Christine's honor at the University of Buffalo Teacher's College where she had not many years before received her doctorate and pioneered in creating computerized programs to teach young children to read. In addition, Jerry actively fostered his daughter Claudia's equestrianism, which matured into a degree as a large animal vet. Weathering the storm was harder for his son Jason, though now he is a very successful periodontist and devoted father living in Raleigh, North Carolina.

Jerry and I sustained ourselves over those hard years by parenting our children, enjoying rewarding careers, and through friendships—largely with other men and with each other. There were and are women too, but that is not what this book is about. Jerry's men friends were and are essentially outdoorsmen—hunting, target-shooting, fishing, and sailing buddies. He's lost quite a few along the way and he makes no bones about saying that he loved them.

Other than Jerry, the men I've loved were cut of very different cloths, but what sewed me to them was a thread at once simple but exceedingly strong that was once invisible to me. Only in the writing of this book, by comparing my ties to those I loved with those I couldn't, did I comprehend what it was made of.

CHAPTER 3

CLARK AND HAROLD,
CLAM CHOWDER AND GEFULTE FISH

IN ADDITION TO food, I've always loved ties. Not family ties, which always seemed obligatory and foisted upon me by random genetic possibilities: No...ties, neckties, cravats. Slim and wide, solid and geometric. Patterned small and patterned large. Silk and wool. Contemporary or vintage. Brightly colorful or somber—expressive of my moods at any moment in time and life. Ties I chose for myself, not chosen or dictated by others or by biology. Neckties I tied myself in a four-in-hand, or half Windsor, of full Windsor. Ties I wore as an expression of who I was or fancied to be. At eighty-five, I no longer wear them, not fancying to be anyone but me.

In the '50s and '60s, across the street from my father's diamond-setting workshop on Nassau Street was a small store called Tie City. Hardly a city. No more than a few phone booths in size, it contained racks and racks of ties of all colors, hues, and materials—some garish, some cautiously conservative, each costing a dollar at the time. When after a hard day of working on jewelry and listening to my father's monologues, I occasionally felt like treating myself before heading home to Queens on subway and bus. I would spend a half hour in Tie City handling the merchandise, looking behind the ties I didn't like for ones I did, and inevitably finding one or two to buy for myself with *my* hard-earned money. On the long subway ride from downtown Fulton Street in Manhattan to Main Street, Flushing, on my way home, I'd peek in the crinkly white bag with *Tie City* emblazoned on it in bold black letters and happily reaffirm the wisdom of my choices.

On rare occasions when my father might feel guilty about something he had said to me like, "Your brother spent a year in college on my hard-earned money and barely passed. Don't think you're going to get away with the same bullshit with me. You're going to college and paying for it and you're staying at home where I can keep my eye on you!" He had similar things to say about my brother's expensive bar mitzvah, for which he barely learned his "Haftorah," the portion of the Torah meant to be chanted and sung in Hebrew. The wedding was another story where S-Head's parents didn't hold up their financial end of the event.

On days like that my father would stop in Tie City and buy a dozen assorted ties, come home, and toss the bag on my bed.

"Here," he'd say, "pick out whatever ones you like."

He liked ties too, though our tastes were very different. Still, he would genuinely try to anticipate what I might like along with the ones he liked. Sometimes he even got it right, but my only retaliatory passive aggressive weapon was to say that I didn't like any.

Then he would pick out one or two. "What about these, I was sure you would like them!"

And I would say, "No, not really," and he would leave them with me and quietly walk out of the room. I still feel guilty about those moments.

In college, I majored in biology. I had no gift for chemistry and no chance of doing well in organic chem, reputed to be the *sine qua non* for entrance into medical school. But I loved biology and excelled in it. I aced comparative anatomy, delighting in the concept of "homologs," but wisely not sharing that delight with my father. I loved the logic of mendelian genetics. But most of all I adored embryology and the man who taught it. Professor Clark D was an expert in the skin patterning of an amphibian called an axolotl, akin to a large salamander. Their embryonic development can be artificially influenced, their maturation advanced, and their skin patterning affected and studied. They also make good pets that rarely nip their feeders.

In addition to his passion for his subject, Clark was a patrician and elegant New Englander who, with his wife Ellie, bred irises, played recorder duets, sailed their own boat in the Long Island Sound, attended Ethical Culture Society meetings on Sundays and enjoyed eating layer cakes that Ellie skillfully baked with forkfuls cut into what seemed like perfect three-quarter-inch cubes.

I know all this because when, a year after graduating from college, I called and asked for a reference for graduate school to get into sociology (my other major), Clark seemed to remember me and invited me to his home for lunch. There was snow on the ground and the brilliantly sunny, plant-filled, glass-enclosed porch blinded and overwhelmed me. Telemann played on their tiny Grundig radio filling the house. A three-course lunch was exquisite, though abstemiously portioned.

When Ellie retreated to do the dishes, Clark asked penetrating questions about my plans like no one before. I was dumbstruck by the scene, answered as best as I could, made up a few answers, and was left at the Mamaroneck train station dazed by what had just taken place. He believed me. He seemed to believe in me. He'd write a letter of support to Columbia and invited me to return sometime in the spring to spend a weekend together sailing, listening to music, and with the promise of more civility. I had no idea that Mamaroneck was a planet in *our* solar system.

No longer living with my parents and my little sister, I spent many spring and summer weekends with Clark and Ellie and came to know the quiet rhythms of them and their cat, Loki.

Ellie planned and executed meals so economically that I learned to smuggle Snickers bars in my overnight bag for after dinner. "Seconds" was a concept previously unknown to them. Nothing was ever wasted. Oil left in a can of sardines would be included in a fish casserole the next day.

Both trained biologists and experienced dissectionists, breakfast could be a particular challenge for me. It often began with each getting half an orange with tiny, serrated spoons made especially for this purpose. It was maddening but I tried. They giggled and I started getting freshly squeezed orange juice with my blueberry pancakes—each with the same number of blueberries. And after every sail, before dinner we each had three Triscuits covered by a thin square of sharp cheddar. The cheese, which might reappear as a one-inch cube served with a wedge of delicious apple pie, all equally and, to my mind, inadequately portioned. A bottle of cold beer would accompany the Triscuits and was intended to last through dinner.

One weekend after sailing, they invited me to a party they attended every August with friends of theirs returning on their schooner from Maine. It was always a dinner of New England clam chowder made with clams they harvested, portions of a wheel of cheddar they sailed with from Maine, and ears of local corn. What made this dinner particularly significant to me was Slats, the captain of the ship, was as well as a prominent sociologist and president of a research foundation. Meeting him could only enhance my future career as a sociologist, which is why Clark and Ellie brought me along.

That afternoon had been particularly windy, and Clark and I went out in a twenty-knot gale. Ellie was fearful that she might get seasick, so she stayed at home. But Clark was an accomplished sailor from childhood, and we did well, at least better than the ship we saw capsize after its mast snapped. Its two sailors were rescued by a nearby boat, but Clark and I felt all the more accomplished when we docked. Though the wind was strong, the August day was hot and very dry. So were we when we disembarked.

Skipping the usual apportioned snack and bottle of cold beer, we showered and dressed for dinner at their friends' Mamaroneck home. Larger and less plant-festooned than Clark and Ellie's, it had the very comfortable feel of old New England money with lots of nautical artifacts here and there. I was told that there were eight invited for dinner at six for seven. I had no comprehension of what that meant but just tagged along in carefully selected and ironed white pants, a white shirt, white tennis shoes, and a yellow wool tie that was not from Tie City, but rather a tweedy men's store in Greenwich Village. The label said that the tie was woven by a tribe called Los Wigwam Weavers in a village somewhere other than Greenwich. I loved the tie, but it wasn't one to be worn on a hot summer's evening, even with ceiling fans spinning above.

Offered a gin and tonic, I gladly accepted, not really knowing what it contained. The size of the frosted glass was closer to suitability for a slushy at 7-Eleven than a before-dinner drink on an empty stomach. I gulped it down, watching the piece of lime in it bob up and down in unison with my Adam's Apple— what Clark and Ellie would probably have called my *laryngeal prominence.*

When the guests were called to the dining room, I bobbed up with much greater alacrity than the time Jerry and I were at the beach observing an unusual mating ceremony. I was even more eager to get some food in my gut. But despite my eagerness, the room was now spinning in unison with the ceiling fans. And my *urinary prominence* (a.k.a. bladder) desperately needed emptying (deprominencement?). Fortunately, the loo was positioned between the living and dining rooms, and while the others took their assigned seats, I congratulated myself for making it as far as the loo, where I proceeded to leisurely pee all over my white pants.

I panicked. Towels, towels, waving towels. No hairdryer, no window to climb out of. I reconciled myself to whatever could possibly come next. Slowly opening the door, I realized that the chair closest to the loo was the only one unoccupied. To the extent that I could, I reasoned that while the guests were babbling about New England seaports and schooners, I could simply slip into that seat, and by the time dinner was over I'd be home and dry.

I followed my plan perfectly and suavely slipped into my seat, feeling an enormous and well-earned relief even greater than the one I'd experienced a few moments prior in the loo. Smiling inwardly, it occurred to me that the room had suddenly gone silent. Everyone was looking at me, though not at my still-wet pants. What had grabbed their attention was my yellow tie in my white soup bowl possibly feeding the entire tribe of Wigwam Weavers. The chowder rose slowly, probably in unison with my blushing realization.

Fortunately, I remember nothing else of that evening. Who knows how high I could have risen with a reference from Slats? I didn't ask for one. Graciously, Clark and Ellie never mentioned it. Tragically, Los Wigwam Weavers shared the fate of other tribes destroyed by New England chowder makers.

Clark and I continued to sail together until he told me that he loved me, but not in the way that I had grown to love him. He revealed to me how unhappy he was sexually with Ellie and how much he was attracted to me. He said Ellie knew. I felt awful, was utterly confused about what to do, and ultimately felt relieved when Clark retired relocated to Hawaii. I heard from him once or twice. He said they were very happy there and sent pictures of their tropical garden.

A few years later, Clark came to New York to attend a conference and telephoned to ask whether I would stay with him in his hotel. I declined as gently as I could. I loved him but was not attracted sexually. Looking back, I hesitate to think that he was grooming me. I just think that he was terribly lonely and starved for the affection his very cautious wife couldn't supply.

Very unlike Clark, Harold was very Jewish. About ten years my senior, we were both single when we met. I was pursuing a master's degree in social work while simultaneously working on my PhD in sociology—both at Columbia. However, by some twist of eleemosynary history, the school of social work was housed in the former Carnegie Mansion on 5th Avenue while Columbia's sociology department was housed at its Upper West Side campus. So geographically and mentally, I shuttled back and forth between social work and sociology.

When we met, Harold was a doctoral (DSW) student in social work, and because I was already a PhD student in sociology, I was taking DSW courses as well. This is all incredibly confusing and somewhat irrelevant though the different statuses we occupied became more relevant and continued to be relevant for many years to come. But, simply stated, we started as friends and classmates.

Though Harold was born and raised in Philadelphia, he managed somehow to live at International House—a residence for many Columbia graduate students from anywhere in the world but Philly. However he pulled that off, he loved living there and befriending as well as dating foreign female students, each one of whom at some point gave him the ultimatum that she would return to her home country unless he would marry them. But that would mean he'd have to leave International House. So, she would move on to another with no apparent bitterness and they'd stay in touch amicably for years. To me, he was just a sweet guy who laughed at my jokes, and maybe at worst, a serial International House dater. Our conversations about women were never prurient, but they were appreciative.

In my first year in social work school, I was blessed with a NIMH fellowship, which covered my tuition and was lucrative enough to ditch my roommate, Arnie, who would never take responsibility for finishing and replacing a container of Häagen-Dazs, leaving instead one pathetic spoonful. This will suffice to explain why we stopped being roomies, but we stopped being friends the day I saw him going through my kitchen knives to see whether I was taking one of his inadvertently.

Entry into every profession as well as established non-professions, involves what the great sociologist Irving Goffman refers to as *degradation ceremonies*. As a delivery boy in the diamond business, I was sent from place to place to purchase a non-existent *diamond-stretcher,* the last of which had unfortunately just been sold, but there was always recommended another place to try if you remained stupid enough to keep trying.

In social work, in order to become a bona fide researcher, I was told that I first had to demonstrate that I could be a practitioner, particularly a caseworker, by doing a one-year placement in a casework setting. That was fine with me. I'd spent a year as a caseworker for the city in child protection. I understood the logic. After all, my previous position did not involve professional supervision.

My placement turned out to be in a highly prestigious social work training unit as a medical social worker in Columbia-Presbyterian Hospital. What I didn't realize until my first day there was that I was the only male student in a unit of fifteen women in a department of thirty-five women that had never had a male social worker in its long and illustrious history.

Instead of a full-length beige coat, which all the other student and staff social workers proudly wore, I was given a much-too-large beige jacket with a social worker badge sewn on my floppy shoulder. The sleeves were so big, when I rolled them up, I resembled Bozo the Clown. Yes, I ultimately became an endowed professor, but I was then and still am a little guy.

The worst part was that the only other hospital staff who wore compulsory uniforms that color were the guys who cleaned the hospital cafeteria, so I was constantly being asked to clean the messes left behind by previous occupants. Likewise, I was not allowed to hang my outer garments in lockers on the fifteenth floor reserved for women social workers and social work students, but in the basement with other cafeteria workers who on occasion asked me what I was doing there and, "What the fuck is a social worker?" Followed up with, "I thought that was a woman's job." Somehow, I never fancied myself a pioneer in quite that way.

What I had most difficulty with, however, was my ability to serve as handmaiden to the doctor, which to me described the desired and idealized relationship between social workers and physicians in the service of patients. Hence, the doctor was always right no matter what you knew about the patient that the doctor didn't. I had no trouble addressing them as "Doctor," but I had trouble listening to accounts of or describing what some distracted doctor mumbled with a reverential, "Doctor says . . ." as though Hippocrates himself had spoken it.

Several of the women in my student unit made it clear that they had chosen medical social work as an option because they hoped to meet and marry a doctor. They routinely flirted with the cute and single ones. Even those who weren't cute. Some of my fellow students might have even been accused of being serial Columbia-Presbyterian doctor daters. I merely wanted to complete my first year as a clinician, so I could get a research placement for my second-year requirement.

My school-assigned supervisor was a genius at psycho-dynamically informed mind games. I'd completed my first semester with an excellent evaluation from her, but at the beginning of my second semester, she called me into her office looking very troubled.

"Mr. Epstein," she said very solemnly, "during the semester break I had occasion to think about your work and, though I gave you a very satisfactory evaluation, I find something missing in your work that I can't quite name and, unless you are able to correct it, I'm afraid you are going to fail both the previous and the current semester. Oh and, by the way, that patient you liked so much and was doing so well—he died over Christmas."

I started crying.

"These things happen Mr. Epstein," she informed me.

Upon closer scrutiny, introspection, and re-examination of all my closed cases, including the patient who died, my nearly fatal flaw surfaced. I did not respect doctors sufficiently. Once that was revealed, a quick change of narrative that included dropping the definite article and calling the doctor simply and reverentially "Doctor" did the trick.

During our end-of-year unit party, where there was a lot to drink, one of the women put her arms around me, looked into my eyes and said, "Irwin, there's something I've been wanting to do from the beginning of our placement." Whereupon she smacked me hard across the face. A veteran social worker, former journalist, and later novelist who observed this asked her why she'd done it. I won't repeat what she answered so as not to demean her, but the social worker told her, "This poor guy has been cooped up here like a rooster in a henhouse for an entire year but told not to touch." Thank you, Marge.

Having successfully run the gauntlet of the doctors and handmaidens in my first-year field placement, I was allowed to do what I originally intended to in my second-year field placement—become a social work researcher. My placement turned out to be pitch-perfect for me—a community organization research placement at Mobilization for Youth, a historic, federally funded, anti-poverty and delinquency-prevention program on Manhattan's Lower East Side. My social work advisor, sponsor, and MFY's research director had arranged it and—of all people—Harold turned out to be my fieldwork supervisor, replacing my dreadful and dread-inducing first-year supervisor. I couldn't have been happier.

What I didn't realize was that my primary research assignment was essentially writing Harold's doctoral dissertation. I didn't really mind. I taught him about Talcott Parsons' systems theory, which I loved, and "Adaptation, Goal-Attainment, Integration and Latent Pattern-Maintenance and Tension Management" theory, which Parsons applied in multiple social contexts from mother-infant dyads to whole societies.

My actual work involved doing what amounted to anthropological field research among neighborhood councils and other voluntary organizations, some of whom benefitted financially and otherwise from MFY's new presence on their neighborhood turf. Several did not and bitterly resented MFY's encroachment, generous funding, and widely positive public attention.

My role was to attend neighborhood meetings uninvited, tell them that I was conducting research with Harold for MFY, and take notes about what they were doing to benefit the neighborhood. The catch here was that those who spoke for MFY had already made it clear that they had no faith in existing local efforts to end poverty and reduce delinquency. MFY offered a better way. Job training, rent strikes, and shaking up the existing networks of social agencies.

It took me a while to figure out that Harold generally sent me to attend meetings of those neighborhood organizations that he chose not to visit, and for good reasons. I became adept at being thrown out of public meetings and accused of being a spy for

MFY. One youth baseball league sponsoring group that nearly a half-century later I still dare not name threatened bodily harm if I ever came back. And these guys meant it.

After we attended our respective meetings, Harold and I would join for dinner in his favorite Lower East Side Jewish dairy restaurant, Ratner's, to talk about the day's events. He always had a strangely gleeful smile when I recounted mine.

In addition to enjoying listening to my tales of expulsion, Harold loved schmoozing with the old Jewish waiters who would attempt to ingratiate themselves by nodding their heads "no" to whatever our first order was, thereby suggesting that whatever it was wasn't fresh, and we should order something else. In that way, they let us know that they were on our side, not Ratner's.

The choice of restaurant was no problem for me; I liked blintzes (as long as they were fresh) and Harold preferred *gefulte* fish, which literally means "stuffed fish," but I never saw it stuffed in an actual fish skin. In actuality, it was chopped fish of various flavor combinations made into a ball, and boiled in fish stock, onions, carrots, and fish bones. The bones produced a gelatinous substance, and the entire mess was served with red beet or white horseradish depending on which side of the Russian Revolution you were on. When brought to the table, Ratner's gefulte looked like a dinosaur egg in a nest of iceberg lettuce, but when reported that it wasn't fresh, Harold settled for the smoked whitefish platter.

We each paid our own way and didn't charge our dinners to MFY. I only say this because the organization subsequently got into a heap of trouble for extra-curricular spending and other indiscretions on the part of its anti-poverty executives. But Harold's and my fiduciary indiscretions were non-existent. We were small potatoes in a very large *latke*.

But back to Harold's fish platter. His were not my choices but *chaque a son gout*. What really bothered me was that he drank his coffee light and always overfilled his cup with milk. Now drinking one's coffee light is hardly a crime, but what bothered me so was that his hands were always a bit shaky, and the coffee always spilled into his saucer and continued to drip from the bottom of his cup through to the strudel. This was a metaphor for nothing at all. But because he was officially my supervisor, I never said anything about it. More significantly, I allowed him to call me Irv—something I've never allowed anyone to do before or since.

Despite that, we got along famously, occasionally attended parties together, and sharing a genuine affection. He dressed the part of a British professor and had a glorious sense of mismatch between tweed jacket, plaid shirt, and wool tie. For the forty-or-so years that I knew him well, I loved his remarkable color sense, though I'd have to say I found him unremarkable intellectually. No matter.

Deep down I think he knew he was rather bland, and as if to compensate he cultivated a surround of characters in the workplace—janitors, errand boys, word processors, anyone who was quirky, irreverent, and could tell a joke. Harold wasn't great at telling jokes; he'd start laughing before the finish line, neutralizing its impact, but he loved it when someone else told one. And you could always rely on him to laugh, stamp a foot, and slap whatever flat surface was nearby.

A confirmed bachelor, he was the benign and loving brother I never had. And though he spoke admiringly of women, and women seemed to love him, I heard rumors years later that he was gay and closeted. Didn't I know?

The atmosphere at MFY was hyper-masculine. The women hires were all remarkably sexy, beautiful, smart, and ideologically left. The latter was necessary but not sufficient. More than rumored to be a ladies' man, our boss was a conspicuously virile and charismatic full professor.

Though born a WASP and son of a minister, Richard affected a kind of beardless Fidelismo style, driving a Jeep, which he enjoyed valet parking at hotels where he might be having a *liaison infidele*. Anything to help the laboring classes.

Richard looked like Elvis but spoke with the drama and persuasiveness of MLK. At the School of Social Work, he conducted a belief-shattering seminar on theories of deviant behavior. To emphasize a point, he would push with one combat boot against the edge of a table, at which Andrew Carnegie may have once dined, and casually flick a cigarette butt out the window into the hedge of what is now the front of the Cooper Hewitt, Smithsonian Design Museum. The women and a few men in the seminar would swoon.

Harold succinctly dubbed him "Bad Boy," but for a brief time, Richard was my idol.

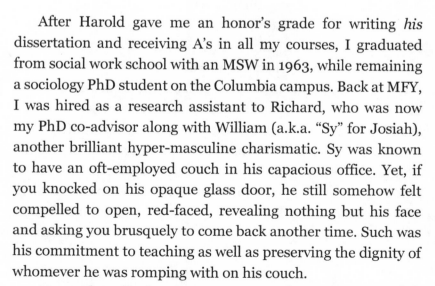

After Harold gave me an honor's grade for writing *his* dissertation and receiving A's in all my courses, I graduated from social work school with an MSW in 1963, while remaining a sociology PhD student on the Columbia campus. Back at MFY, I was hired as a research assistant to Richard, who was now my PhD co-advisor along with William (a.k.a. "Sy" for Josiah), another brilliant hyper-masculine charismatic. Sy was known to have an oft-employed couch in his capacious office. Yet, if you knocked on his opaque glass door, he still somehow felt compelled to open, red-faced, revealing nothing but his face and asking you brusquely to come back another time. Such was his commitment to teaching as well as preserving the dignity of whomever he was romping with on his couch.

At a student-faculty party at Fayerweather Hall, I recall him drunkenly sliding down a very long and shiny wooden banister while an even more famous and famously socially awkward sociologist, nicknamed Bob or RKM, preferred to build a tower of empty beer cans rather than talk with students. They were very different men, and those were very different times. Not all was fun and games however, if you were a student.

Being thrown out of a baseball league meeting on the LES was nothing compared to my being demolished at a meeting in front of sociological idols uptown at the Plaza Hotel during my first post-master's year at MFY, while planning my PhD dissertation research.

I'm not sure what Richard saw in me. We never had a personal talk. But he had me informally interview all perspective research job candidates after he did and asked me what I thought. It seemed strange to me but in retrospect, but I think he saw something about me that I didn't see. I compensated for his blind spot. A sociologist, he was totally a-psychological and had trouble assessing people.

My first formal assignment was to hunt, gather, and organize data about who private social work agencies served and who they wanted to serve. Long before people were thinking about institutional racism, that was my first foray into institutional classism and the way it was justified. I rough-drafted an article that Richard had assigned to me on the theme of social work's abandonment of the poor and the way the quest for professional status affected that. The premise was documenting a shift from concrete service provision and advocacy for the poor to psychotherapy for the middle class. This represented a radical critique of social work's aspiration to be seen as a true profession rather than mere occupation and the price the poor would pay for it.

When I returned to Richard months later, with my combination of handwritten, typed, Xeroxed, and stapled pages, he had it typed, and the next week threw it on my desk the way my father through a bag of Tie City ties on my bed.

What I saw amazed me. On the title page, I was listed as a second author. He would soon present the paper at a conference in Buffalo, but asked if I would be willing to do the same at a much smaller meeting in New York City?

I was starry-eyed. *Are you kidding me?* My first conference presentation and first publication with someone whose brilliant writings (if not his quotidian behavior) I admired enormously? I couldn't believe my luck and my mentor's largesse.

Soon I learned that instead of his presenting the paper at an annual conference in Buffalo, my presentation would take place in a rented suite at the posh Plaza, as far north symbolically from the LES as Buffalo is geographically from NYC. His *day conference* was sponsored by the University of Buffalo School of Social Work. Mine was funded by a special grant from the Rockefeller Foundation.

What I didn't know then was that Arthur, the organizer of my conference, was my mentor's archrival for foundation money in the war against juvenile delinquency. Arthur's magic bullet was equipping delinquent adolescents with tape recorders and having them interview other delinquents. The theory was that through telling their stories and self-reflection they would mend their delinquent ways—if they didn't pawn or flog the tape recorders.

It came as no surprise then that Arthur recorded the conference proceedings for posterity and publication. I was incredibly nervous, trying and failing badly to mimic my mentor's presentation style. Sweating profusely in my new seersucker suit and carefully selected tie, I noticed that when I finished, Art turned off his recorder.

I returned to my seat, so relieved that it was over and apprehensive about questions other esteemed professors might throw at me. Instead, the question-and-answer period was pre-empted by Arthur, who railed about my mentor's cowardice in sending a lackey in his place. This was followed by a set of dead-on impersonations of my mentor and a female co-author of his, whom many believed to be sleeping with him. (They later divorced their respective spouses and married. I was not asked to be ringbearer.)

Shaken by this excoriation by proxy, at the sumptuous lunch break I was approached by one or three rare empathic and elite social scientists who consoled me while I tried to raise a fantastic crab-salad sandwich to my trembling lips and not stain my tie. No gefulte fish at the Plaza. I remember the names of these kind souls and their words of comfort more than the sandwich.

The next day, I stomped into my mentor's office opening with, "You'll never believe what happened yesterday!"

Stolidly but with a slight corner smile, he said, "I figured that might happen, but I thought it would be a good experience for you." I'm proud to say that I gave him the finger and left his office. He remained my mentor, sponsor, and co-dissertation advisor, and for that I remain grateful to him. But he was no longer my idol. In retrospect, I realize that he never looked me in the eyes.

At my PhD defense, which concerned the effect of professionalization on social workers' political beliefs and actions, he didn't show. He sent a message to Sy, my co-chair, saying it was the finest dissertation he'd read. The next day, I confirmed with his secretary that he'd been shacked up with someone at an UES hotel.

Bad Boy indeed.

Harold and I remained friends over the years, and he was instrumental in my longed-for return to Manhattan and what was then known as Hunter College School of Social Work on the UES near art galleries and the Metropolitan Museum, where I occasionally nipped off for afternoon lectures from Karl Haas or courses on German expressionism. Harold became chair of the doctoral program in which I taught research and supervised dissertations.

At the time, I was still married to my second wife, Kayla, but things were not going well between us. There was little fun in our lives—mostly illness and discord. At the beginning of my first fall semester, the elevator door opened on the level where my office was and I noticed a tanned, androgynous (my weakness), loquacious, and charming (my preference) young woman sitting on the floor in active and clearly enjoyable conversation with a gaggle of other students—male and female. She wore fuchsia clamdiggers and sandals, and obviously had spent time at the beach. My first thought was, *This is a woman who knows how to have fun.* Several years later, Fran and I were married, something I've never regretted. And at this writing, having spent thirty years together, much of it with her bravely battling cancer, she still knows how to have fun.

But in the late 70's and early 80's, Kayla and I were still married. And now, so was Harold to Judy. And in an astonishing coincidence, the four of us were having dinner together in the Caucuses, an UES Russian restaurant, when in walked Fran with her then-husband and a small group of other couples, clearly good friends. Fran and I nodded hellos of recognition, but nothing more. Years later, she and I realized that was the night Fran and her ex-husband, Stanley, were informing friends that they were splitting.

Some Yiddish speakers would say that that coincidence was not simply a random event or even synchronicity but an indication that she and I were meant to be—*bashert.* But what I remember most about that night was hearing Harold's wife make disparaging remarks about gay men and seeing Harold laugh. It left me utterly confused, still unknowing about Harold's sexual history and thinking about Clark and his closeted unhappiness.

I never asked Harold about any of this, and we remained largely office friends until he died of bladder cancer. Shortly before, when he had already retired, he came to my office with an apology. The apology was not for exploiting me as a graduate student. In fact, later in life he would introduce me at parties as "the guy who wrote my dissertation for me." The apology was for reassigning the dissertation seminar to himself after several years of my teaching it quite successfully. He said he never should have done that. I told him quite sincerely that it didn't matter, and he had no reason to feel guilty about it.

What I am left with is profound sadness for how Harold and Clark each might have suffered sexually, though we never discussed it. I never wear ties anymore, but my loving memories of Harold are sustained in part by two ties that his wife, Judy, gave me on my request after he died. Reading the labels today for the first time, I see they were not woven by Los Wigwam Weavers in America's Southwest. (I never thought they were.) Instead, they were woven by Shetland Weavers from Loch Carron in the Scottish Highlands. Neither have ever been near a bowl of New England clam chowder, and if I have anything to do with it, they never will. But Harold always loved that story about my tie in my soup and stamped his foot and slapped his desk each time he asked me to retell it.

CHAPTER 4

LARRY, IN LIFE AS IN RESEARCH

(1945-1996)

IN SEPTEMBER 1968, I began my academic career as an assistant professor at the prestigious University of Michigan School of Social Work in idyllic Ann Arbor. Recruited there by my friend, Tony T, who will appear later, I thought it the perfect job for me in the perfect place for my newly created family. It wasn't. But that was neither my family nor Tony's fault.

My problem was the Midwest. And though I missed Manhattan every day I was in Ann Arbor, it took me thirteen years to return. It was only students like Larry who made teaching at U of M tolerable.

Let me be clear. My first wife, Lyn, and I had been happy to leave Manhattan. Who knew what my four-month-old son, Dan, was thinking? Now he can't wait to spend time in New York. But in 1968, one sunny and hot August Saturday, Lyn and I took Dan to Riverside Park for a cooling and relaxing stroll by the Hudson—he in a fragile fold-up stroller. We were both tense and excited about the move, but mostly excited to escape our families of orientation—at least I was. Returning to our eleventh floor UWS apartment, I noticed the door was unlocked and slightly ajar. Trying not to be my father, who would immediately think the worst, I assumed that there must be a plumbing problem in our kitchen that our super had discovered and was fixing while we were out. Incredible!

Once inside, though, I found a very big man who looked nothing like our super emerging from our bedroom with tools in hand, saying, "I swear I didn't take anything," as he passed through the broken apartment door heading for the back stairs. I was still thinking that the problem must have been in our bathroom when Lyn started shouting that he had taken her Lapis and diamond engagement ring that my father had crafted for her at my request.

Incensed and stupid, I got into the waiting elevator thinking I might somehow intercept the robber at lobby level and retrieve the ring through peaceful negotiation and, perhaps, an offering of a cash reward. Running outside in hopes of finding a policeman, I was immediately relieved to see a police car with two officers inside drinking their coffees and eating glazed donuts. I ran to the closest open window and told the cop in the passenger seat that we had just been robbed, that the robber (sorry, the "alleged perpetrator") was still in the stairwell, and they should arrest him so I could retrieve my wife's ring.

Looking at each other quizzically, they carefully covered their coffees, folded their paper napkins around their partially eaten donuts, placed them in their respective Dunkin' Donuts bags, ambled out of their car, loudly sighed in unison, and reluctantly followed me inside. Drawing their guns, they encouraged me to lead the way up the back stairwell, instructing me to walk up slowly and if I "see the guy and recognize him" to let them know and they would cuff him.

"Are you nuts?" I said. "You go first, and I'll be right behind *you!*"

"Okay," they unenthusiastically murmured and slowly set out.

By the time we reached floor eleven, it was evident to all three of our keen investigative minds that the thief had already escaped and very likely ran out the lobby and crossed the street in front of their patrol car while they were unwrapping their crullers.

Once in our apartment, after reholstering their guns, they interviewed both my shaken wife and me while I caught my breath. After taking our best description of the thief and the ring, the lead investigator said that there was, "no chance in hell that we would ever see that ring again." Lyn began to cry.

With an air of obvious disdain toward me, he said, "I know if it were *me* and the *perp* was still in the apartment, I would have held him while my wife called the police."

"Are you kidding me?" I said. "This guy was a head taller than me, had burglary tools, and I've got a wife and baby here in a stroller."

To which he shrugged and replied, "Don't you have any tools, a hammer or something?" *Thank you, officers, have a great day.*

That sealed it. We were both happy to get the hell out of Manhattan and with great relief drove directly to Ann Arbor with a burbling kid on a mattress in the back of the old black Buick convertible my father-in-law had given us as our only wedding present, thankfully without first painting it bright red.

———◇———

When we passed through Detroit, the fire engines were already out. It was August of 1967, the time of the Detroit Riots or the Detroit Uprising as they have later come to be called. Our getting lost in Detroit was a particular problem because all the street names were French but pronounced with the flat Midwestern local dialect. I'd been a French literature minor in college, so my special efforts in asking directions and calling streets as I thought they should be called only elicited strange looks and incorrect directions. To me, the majestically burning Livernois Street was *Leevernywah* while the locals pronounced it *Livver-noise*. Nonetheless, we got directions that gradually found us to our destination.

When we arrived in Ann Arbor hours later than expected, we were hot and exhausted and hungry. I had a list of recommended restaurants that my new colleagues had provided for us. Easy choice. The old reliable—Chinese. The eponymous Leo Ping's was the only—but highly recommended—Chinese joint in town. Welcoming air-conditioned comfort and familiar Formica tables, we settled the kid in a highchair and looked up to discover a blond, blue-eyed cheerleader of a server carrying a basket of assorted bakery rolls and butter. "Hi, you guys," she welcomed us. "I'll bring you your complementary salads in a moment. Would you like French, Russian, or Thousand Island with them?" We'll revisit this Midwestern trinity of salad dressings in a later chapter, but we were mystified. This was not a scene that had ever taken place in my cherished Hoo Lok Corporation Restaurant in New York's Chinatown. Turning to my engagement-ringless bride and mother of my child, I said, "I think we've made a very big mistake."

My career miscalculation became evident even before the semester began. I was invited to an emergency meeting of research faculty to respond to the crisis in Detroit. This was my chance to informally join the research faculty as colleague rather than job applicant. I was excited. To my chagrin, it soon became clear that my colleagues viewed the crisis as an opportunity to apply for a research grant to study the socio-political attitudes of Detroiters vis-à-vis the tragic burning, widespread looting, and massive dislocation through what was already known as The Detroit Area Study. By contrast, Wayne State University School of Social Work faculty were finding food, shelter, and medical services for displaced Detroiters.

Though I was hired primarily as a researcher, I was also a human being. For years I wondered whether I should have applied for a job at Wayne State, but as a sociology PhD from Columbia, I'm not sure they would have hired me. At U of M, I was welcomed as a first-born son.

The intersection between culinary and career miscalculation became apparent over the next several months as we received invitations to different faculty members' homes for dinner. People were uniformly nice, though homes were stratified by assistant, associate, and full professorships. The dinners, however, were remarkably the same—overdone roast beef, mashed potatoes, and overcooked string beans. *What is this?* I thought. *Everyone's more or less opposed to the Vietnam war. Good! But what's with the food?*

Still, we were appreciative of our welcome. We decided to reciprocate all our previous invitations with a Sunday brunch in a spirit of generosity as well as early training in culinary diversity. The buffet centered on a self-serve, Cajun shrimp and rice dish made with the special seasoning I'd carefully brought with me from New York and cooked in a yellow Le Creuset casserole we'd received as a wedding present. Starting with the trinity of onions, green bell pepper, and celery, I prepared it with jumbo shrimp, which cost one dollar a piece. I'd found them in Ann Arbor's lively Saturday farmers' market, where academics and their spouses of all ranks, social standings, and genders would meet and shop as though equals. The jumbo shrimp, however, were equal to none in size and will re-appear, shrimp by shrimp, in my chapter about Tony T.

For all my efforts to alter our social environment to suit us, our marriage was falling apart, so I accepted a Fulbright to Wales hoping that we might be able to save the marriage in a more interesting cultural venue. After claiming that she wanted to live in Europe, Cardiff wasn't European enough and didn't appeal to Lyn. Very reluctantly, I went alone. Though the local food was a disaster—peas, chips, sausage, and spaghetti on toast—it opened my mind and heart to the world beyond New York City.

In any town in bucolic Wales or industrial UK you could still find a decent Chinese and Indian restaurant. Most importantly, I found like-minded, culturally diverse friends and worldly colleagues. Since my bed-sit was too small, I made dinner parties for them—cooking at their places.

By then Lyn and I added a daughter, Rebecca (Becs). Very much a major part of their care from the start, I missed them terribly while I was abroad. And it was awkward explaining to people why my family had not come along. I still have the letters I wrote to my kids from Cardiff, with drawings of three-wheeler cars for the disabled, and the castles I visited, and curved streets with curved houses and curved doorways.

Upon my return, Lyn and I became the first couple in Michigan history to be granted dual custody. What an achievement.

After a year of shuttling the kids back and forth to our respective homes, Lyn moved to LA to find herself and write a book called *Mothercare* about being a single mother, emphasizing the importance of exercise, diet, and meditation— all far ahead of its time. She neglected to mention that at the time of the writing, the children were living with me. For the eight years until I remarried, I was a single father to my children— which was particularly gratifying to me but challenging in Ann

Arbor, since all the single parents I knew were women who were pissed at their ex-husbands about inadequate child support, irregular childcare, and mainly about just them being men. I was a rare but not terribly exotic fish swimming in a small collegiate pond surrounded by single mothers who were now staunchly feminist sharks. Still, I loved taking care of my kids much as I had loved taking care of my sister. And because I had a steady income, was not reliant on financial support from my ex-spouse, and enjoyed a flexible academic work schedule, I was indeed privileged in comparison to many other single women parents.

Still, I experienced a unique form of housing discrimination in very liberal Ann Abor. A university town provides plenty of sabbatical homes to rent, but few willing to rent to a single father with kids. One particularly piquant rejection came from a well-known and widely published feminist who wondered aloud whether, as a single father, I could keep her not remarkably tidy home the way she did. "Who does the cleaning for you?" she asked. "Do you know how to vacuum? What about hiring my cleaning woman?"

I said I could afford that monthly, but she meant weekly. *Forget it, lady.*

For several years, I had an ongoing romantic relationship with Maryanne, an open-hearted, beautiful woman and former student. Though we loved each other, and she loved my kids who loved her, she wasn't ready to take on the roles and responsibilities of stepmother or even live-in girlfriend. The ups and downs with her were both beautiful and painful and only ended when she developed an autoimmune disease after being hit by a car. She went on to marry someone who could take care of her. I could not. But when I met Kayla, the woman who was to become my second wife, Maryanne stopped seeing my kids. This was their second major maternal loss. Fortunately, for me there were my men friends.

Larry, known to his wife, Ikie, as "Llah," was my first truly loving friendship with a male student. What attracted me to Larry was that he was the funniest and most irreverent man I had ever met, and his appearance in my classroom represented a newfound joy in my stressful personal life. Tall, with a shock of kinky and unruly black hair, big Fu Manchu mustache, thick glasses in front of glazed eyes, gap-toothed smile, pigeon-toed shuffle, and loose-limbed upper body, Larry always looked like a basketball player about to receive a pass and take a fadeaway jump shot. There was good reason for it. For all his awkward ambling about, he was a remarkably good player. But rather than taking the off-court instruction from his coach, Larry was receiving off-court instructions from a satellite captained by Mel Brooks somewhere in space.

Positioning himself in the back of the room where I taught a required master's research course, he was one of the many who registered for it only because he had to. Social work MSW students are notorious for trying every strategy to avoid research courses—and that's precisely the reason I loved teaching them. In my long and extensively published career, perhaps my most cited paper was entitled, "Pedagogy of the Perturbed: Teaching Research to the Reluctants." Published in the early '80s, in one section I wrote about the importance of humor in teaching these courses, for students as well as instructors. In another, I wrote about the importance of demanding precision in the use of language. My paper drew upon examples from actual student papers and course evaluations. One student wrote a paper about "working with people living in abstract poverty." Another proposed "exploring the anals of deceased administrators." And how does one defend oneself against a student evaluation that says, "The professor spoke too precisely to be readily understood." There's something about that which will stay in my heart forever.

Larry and I understood each other perfectly from the moment we met—both New Yorkers, both collectors of human foibles, and both possessed of an irresistible desire to poke holes in pretension. I don't know where he got that, but I know where I did. One day in class, I was struggling to make the wonder of the Chi-square statistic and its many applications as thrilling to my students as it was to me. Sensing the gap between my enthusiasm and the class's complete boredom, Larry leaned back in his chair as far as he could possibly go, raising his hand with a certain urgency.

Relieved at a break in the deadness, I recognized him. "Uh, Professor Epstein," he offered, "with all due respect, in your discussion of Chi-square, I wonder whether you are factoring in the Zeigarnik effect?"

Seizing on his question, I first grabbed some chalk, then thanked him for the excellent question and began writing phony mathematical equations on the blackboard, making a point to break several pieces of chalk as I did. Then when I was at serious risk of no longer maintaining a straight face, I suggested that perhaps the question was too sophisticated for the rest of the class, and we could discuss it after.

That moment cemented our friendship for the rest of his all-too-short life.

From that day forward, I had a play-pal in Ann Arbor. Never taking advantage of our student-teacher relationship, every paper he wrote was exquisitely wrought, research-perfect, but topically nonsensical—each one beginning with the phrase, "In life as in research." That phrase came back to humble me years later when, as a research consultant at Mount Sinai, where I routinely critiqued clinical trial methods, I was pleased each time my wife, Fran, was accepted into a clinical trial.

Back in Michigan, the final assignment I gave to my research classes was always the same. Design a research study that you would like to carry out that will produce findings relevant to your social work interests. Larry's final paper offered a meticulously designed, gold-standard, randomized controlled study involving the use of aversive interventions, such as electric shocks, to teach students who hated research to love it. The paper was filled with mock tables and graphs, demonstrating that no matter how much they were punished for it, students still hated research. That paper was technically and conceptually perfect. Submission to a university's ethics committee, however, would have had us both out on our asses, but I can assure the reader that research standards were never compromised by either of us.

We later broke the law by smoking grass together, but our research standards remained uncompromised. So, while much of my career involved welcoming the challenge of teaching the courses that students didn't want to take, to me success was achieved when I received evaluations like, "I thought I would hate this course but I didn't." It's a low bar I know, but challenging circumstances call for strategic compromise.

Larry moved to Ann Arbor in 1968 with his witty and beautiful wife Eileen, known generally as "Ikie," whom he'd met as a teenager at summer camp. Apparently, she'd received her sobriquet when, as a bald infant, someone in her family had said she looked exactly like President Dwight D. "Ike" Eisenhower. I can testify that as an adult, she looked nothing like Ike and still doesn't. I can understand completely why he fell in love with her, but the reverse remained something of a mystery. In her seventies now, Ikie is still quite beautiful and funny, a grandmother and now an accomplished painter in Portland, Oregon. But in Ann Arbor, they were a threesome living with their dog, Estelle Goldberg. This is one of the few places in the book that I will reveal any character's full name.

I'm not sure what I taught Larry, but I know he taught me how to roll a joint. He was great with my kids, who were little then, and he'd often play guitar and sing original songs to them. One that's hard to forget is "Pickin' My Nose." The melody eludes me, but the lyrics linger even today, because those are the only lyrics—with the occasional, "Just," inserted at the beginning of a new stanza for dramatic effect.

We had so much fun together, the three or four or five or six of us, depending on how you counted Estelle. When the three of them moved back to Brooklyn, I mourned but couldn't possibly resent it. I'd wished they had taken me and my two kids with them. But Ann Arbor was a relatively benign place to raise my children alone. The public school to which they could walk was excellent and, for better or for worse, populated almost entirely with children of academics. My daughter, Becs, knew and used the word *sabbatical* in kindergarten. When, in 1973, I took them to England with me, she referred to it as *her* sabbatical.

Larry and Ikie and I remained in touch after they left Ann Arbor. Estelle wasn't much of a correspondent, but she was affectionate when we visited for my son Dan's fifth birthday. The trip was sold as a birthday trip for him so I could take him to the Museum of Natural History. At the time he was a dinosaur nut and, though by no means a paleontologist, still is. That trip was so memorable for him that he recently returned to the museum to celebrate the fiftieth anniversary of his screaming fit occasioned by his claim that a particular dinosaur skeleton was incorrectly labelled. A guard made me take him out of the exhibit screaming and kicking. I'm relieved to say that upon his return he acknowledged that he was wrong but never found the guard to whom he needed to apologize. He's matured.

What I remember most about that visit was the road trip Larry and I took together from Brooklyn to Manhattan to see a rock concert. I have no recollection of where or who performed, but I remember a particular traffic light that we stopped at in his little VW. Larry was driving and we'd each taken a few tokes before we left Ikie and Estelle watching Dan. The grass took effect on both of us exactly as that light turned from green to red. Time stood still and the light remained red. To us, it appeared as though the light remained red for hours. We discussed the possibility of our exchanging seats several times, but I didn't want to drive in Manhattan. We couldn't stop laughing. I'm not sure we even went to a concert, but that was both the shortest and longest road trip we ever took together.

I helped Larry get a job as a community organizer at Mobilization for Youth, where I had worked years before. Harold was still there at the time and had worked his way up the chain of command. My former mentor was no longer there because of the financial scandal, and a close friend of Harold's was now Executive Director. But the Lower East Side was not yet as hip and happening. Poverty, delinquency, and drug addiction were still major problems.

My letter of support for Larry's candidacy as a community organizer was a masterpiece of double-entendres disguised as praise. Only Larry and I knew just how funny it was. But he got the job and Harold loved having him around. To Harold, Larry was a 'wild man', but to me, just a sweet and very funny guy.

Larry's MFY job was to help organize rent strikes in local tenement buildings where absentee landlords were not providing adequate services or dealing with health and safety issues. Many were rumored to be paying off NYC housing inspectors.

Larry did a fine job and fully believed in his and the organization's mission. Unfortunately, he stirred up more than a hornet's nest when he submitted to the *Journal of Social Work* an article entitled, "The Origin of the Feces" about his effort to organize a building in which two families were warring about whether the small pile of shit left in the hallway between their apartments originated from one party's dog or the other's kid. To make matters worse, one family was Black and the other

Puerto Rican. As they were hurling insults at each other, Larry's effort to persuade them to stop fighting and join in withholding rent from the greedy landlord floundered until he offered to clean up the mess himself.

It gets worse. Larry could do accents. So, he captured the exchanges between parties in Black, Puerto Rican, and White liberal Jewish vernacular, complete with bilingual curses. The amazing part of this story is that several members of this most important, peer-reviewed journal in the self-proclaimed profession of social work wanted to publish it. It's true, it reeked of verisimilitude. Others claimed racism and threatened to resign from the editorial board if it was published. Ultimately the paper was rejected. My guess is he listed it on his C.V. as *unpublished paper*.

Larry became despairing about the possibilities of community organizing in NYC, and he, Ikie, and Estelle pulled up stakes and relocated to Portland, Oregon, where he'd secured a teaching job at Portland State School of Social Work. I'd written another stellar reference letter for him as now did Harold. Mine was multilayered of course. Despite my reference duplicity, I absolutely believed that Larry would make a great teacher and that students would adore him as I did.

I couldn't have been more mistaken.

Larry's West Coast students did not appreciate Larry's East Coast humor the way I did. In fact, they found his antics, his accents, and his jokes offensive enough to boycott his classes and protest his rehiring. This was terribly hard and disappointing to him as well as to me. To my utter surprise he enrolled in Lewis and Clark Law School.

I couldn't imagine him in law school. Then again, over dinner at a social work conference in Atlantic City we argued whether the word was *litigious* or *litiginous*. When our server asked what she could get us, he asked for a thesaurus. She thought it was a kind of fish and said she'd ask chef. She returned saying, "Sorry, all out." Maybe chef thought it was a fish as well. But that could have been the beginning of his legal career.

Over the years he continued to harass me. Having published a research paper redundantly entitled, "Advocates on Advocacy" about social workers' case and class advocacy efforts and techniques, he sent me a congratulatory letter on letterhead he fabricated from the "Avocado Growers Association of America" praising and thanking me for my current research promoting the consumption of avocados in the United States. I wrote back thanking him and his organization, saying how much their support meant to me. He wrote back asking for a major contribution.

Ultimately Larry became a land-use judge, adjudicating proposals to place community mental health facilities in NIMBY neighborhoods that opposed them. The strategy he employed in his "Origins" paper was of no use in this context, though the conflicts were just as ugly. But this time, with legal authority and sound social values on his side, he did good and did well. Though I wouldn't have wanted to see him in the courtroom for fear I would be ejected for laughing when our eyes met over a defendant's patently hypocritical testimony or a lawyer's pompous bloviating in the interest of making money or protecting property values.

We remained in regular telephone contact over the years, and I always thought Larry was a bit of a hypochondriac. In retrospect, I wonder whether I didn't take his complaints seriously enough. Then I received a phone call that didn't sound like him. He telephoned to say that he had a rare form of cancer—sarcoma of the lungs. My first thought was all the pot he'd smoked and Paraquat, a carcinogenic herbicide sprayed over marijuana fields in Mexico under the direction of the Reagan Administration.

For good reasons, he was frightened. He and Ikie had two

children by now. We spoke regularly and he even chatted with Fran, the wife he and Ikie had never met but who was by then a veteran fighter of cancer and the survivor of a bone marrow transplant. She remembers him in conversation as not being funny but being very dear and solicitous of her health troubles. What I remember was his sounding at peace when he began receiving hospice care at home. I have no memory of how I learned he died, but it is a loss I still deeply feel. I'm glad my children and my wife each knew him and a different part of him in their own way.

A few years ago, I met a Danish research professor named Lars at an international conference in Helsinki at which we were giving plenary presentations. Looking not in the least like Larry, Lars had that familiar glint in his eyes. My first comment to him was, "So, Lars, you are from Denmark, that means you must love herring."

His instant enthusiastic and prideful response was, "I am the only Dane in the entire country who hates herring!" Over the past few years, giving and attending each other's talks in various countries, I've gotten to know Lars better through our very silly email harassment of each other. Recently, I was shocked to learn that Lars also hates cheese of any kind, which, if they had the death penalty in Denmark, would make him eligible for it. Still, Lars claims that he and a small band of fellow Danish anti-cheesers established an association for *cheese deniers*—a minority group being under a heavy societal pressure. But he reassured me, "We are strong." Lars and Larry would have loved each other.

Lars claims that with the advent of Danish crime and political series on Netflix, there are a growing number of Americans showing up in Denmark thinking they speak Danish.

By applying ridiculous efforts at Danish accents to English
sentences they render their sentences totally incomprehensible
in any language.

Concerned that I might not do justice to my allusion to Lars in
this book, he volunteered the following: *"Lars, den eneste dansker
som indrømmer, at han hader sild og enhver form for ost."*

How I would have loved hearing Larry render it.

CHAPTER 5

TERRY, THE ARACHNOPHILE

YEARS OF TEACHING have taught me that in a square-tabled classroom, there are three seats to pay special attention to—the one directly opposite me, the one behind the one directly opposite me, and the one immediately to my right. The latter seat was almost always occupied by a woman who wanted to be my helpmate in some way—not sexual, just helpful. A daddy's girl?

Inevitably, it seemed the ones directly opposite were always occupied by men who wanted to compete with me for leadership and authority in the classroom. It's as though they want to reverse positions and have the entire class turn to them for their wisdom and cleverness. One example is Tony G who I will describe at length later.

In addition to research methods, I taught a required course in complex organizations at Michigan. As a budding sociologist, I was thrilled to have the opportunity to teach a course in organizational theory, since the curriculum of no other school of social work in the country offered what, to me, was an essential course for all future social workers.

My first lecture of my first offering of the course occurred in the fall of 1968. I introduced myself humbly and then with great fanfare introduced my hero, the great German sociologist and father of organizational theory, Max Weber (1864-1920). In my opening and thoroughly rehearsed lecture, I spoke passionately about the importance of social workers' understanding of bureaucracies even though I knew many aspired to be private practitioners in their own plant-filled, colorfully carpeted offices. Like Freud's. That was long before managed care and its complex bureaucratic elements crept in under the rug.

I was elaborating on the famous (and in leftist circles, the later infamous) Harvard sociologist Talcott Parsons' translation of Weber from the original German. Wading through Parson's incredible, two-page footnote elaborating on Weber's distinction between the *professional* and the *bureaucrat,* Andrea sitting directly to my right gave forth an enormously visible and audible yawn. It's one thing to yawn discreetly in a seat somewhere else in the classroom. But next to the lecturer and facing the entire class makes another statement entirely.

This guy is a total, effing bore! Maybe I was.

I turned to the student who later became Andi and asked, "Do I bore you?" That was the beginning of a lifelong friendship and colleagueship, which I cherish to this day. But this book is about men I've loved, not about women I love.

Back in the classroom, I came to learn that those who sat *behind* the chair directly opposite me were not my competitors. They wanted to separate or distinguish themselves from the rest of the class—neither out of arrogance nor superiority but out of practiced marginality. They were the renegades, half-in, half-out, the guys I was most curious about. Larry was one. Terry was another. In my own way, I suppose, I am another.

That's where Larry sat in my first research class at Michigan and that's where Terry sat a few years later. This time, however, the course was complex organizations. Unlike Larry, Terry was not in the least funny. He asked seriously complex and brilliant questions in a quiet, unprepossessing voice almost as though talking between his teeth. Not menacing, but otherwise looking like a typical 70s biker—blond ponytail, blond beard, black leather jacket, black jeans, black T-shirt, motorcycle boots, and aviator glasses.

There was no sense that he was interested in striking up a friendship or combatting with me. Moreover, it was almost as though his intelligence manifested itself despite itself. Plus, he sounded like a Detroiter, not a New Yorker. New Yorkers often hung around after class to ask what borough I was from or what elementary school I attended and to tell me about themselves. Terry would ask a terrific question at the end of class, applying organizational theory to one agency context or another—prison, mental hospital, half-way house—until he got his answer and quickly and unobtrusively exited the room.

I was intrigued and asked a couple of colleagues whether they knew who he was, but no one did or showed much interest. So, after a few more weeks of being intrigued by his questions and the contradiction between his mild demeanor and ominous outfit, I became curious to go to the admissions office, where I pulled his application folder and discovered that he had a PhD in linguistics and had been an assistant professor of linguistics at USC with several publications about Indonesian grammatical structures on his CV. This guy's getting a master's degree in social work in Ann Arbor? It made no sense to me.

Without hesitation on my end but considerable hesitation on his, I decided to find out who the hell he was. What was his story? After we became friends, I learned he'd been bored teaching linguistics, left his teaching job to pursue other interests, started writing a novel, feigned mental illness to avoid the Vietnam War, and wound up in a half-way house in Los Angeles where he saw social workers from that perspective, and though he didn't especially like them, he liked what they did.

Terry and I became intimate friends while working together in a tutorial course that I had agreed to sponsor. It was a study which made use of his knowledge of linguistics and mine of clinical research. This was the time when neuro-linguistic programming (NLP) was first introduced into psychotherapy, principally by Richard Bandler and John Grinder's 1976 two volume, curiously titled and psychedelically book-jacketed, *The Structure of Magic: A Book about Language and Therapy.*

In a precursor to a social work research method that I refined and later called "Clinical Data-Mining" in a 2009 book published by Oxford Press, Terry and I applied Bandler and Grinder's theory of how people frame their problems with metaphors concerning the predominate of their five senses. The theory was if you determined their dominant sense metaphor, you could use it to reprogram people's minds. Today it's a big business and the theoretical forerunner of Tony Robbins' pitching Americans to "take immediate control of [their] mental, emotional, physical and financial destin[ies]."

Here, it's important to note that Terry was not attempting to use NLP in social work practice. Nor was I encouraging him to. If anything, I thought the theory was rubbish. Our effort was far less ambitious or activist. It was merely to see whether the texts of clients' presentations of self and their problems conformed to what Bandler and Grinder claimed and how consistently they did, e.g., were people who said things like, "I see what you're saying" consistently visual in the metaphorical choices they make in their self-narratives.

Now that study could be done easily by computers that read and categorize text. Then, it meant Terry and I had to read the texts and independently code them into categories based on Bandler and Grinder's typology. Like Larry's no-finding mock study, our study results were equally unimpressive and negated, if not mocked, Bandler and Grinder's theory. At least in our sample, the theory didn't hold. Nonetheless, if I, like many other social workers and a few hucksters, had jumped on the NLP bandwagon, I could have been a rich man today. But like good researchers, Terry and I *followed the data* and discovered a rich and meaningful friendship as a result.

In Ann Arbor, though student and professor, Terry and I spent lots of free time together. He had a live-in girlfriend, Robyn, who was easy about sharing Terry's time. They even welcomed babysitting my kids one weekend when Maryanne and I went to Toronto. Terry took my son, Dan, to his first hockey game. Later Terry and I attended a Linda Ronstadt concert together and fell in love with the same woman while Robyn watched the kids. What cads we were!

Though he was a Detroiter, Terry loved California. His relocation to LA was a great loss to me but we remained in contact. An amateur naturalist, he loved spending time camping in national parks and climbing in Joshua Tree Monument. The only regret he ever expressed to me was that he did not pursue a PhD in arachnology. He loved spiders and other creepy crawlers. Once when I visited him in LA, he asked me to be sure to not to accidentally step on his house pet Wooly, the ten-inch, black, wooly tarantula that was hiding under his couch in the living room. *No worries, you two.*

Terry had a house—really a shack with an outhouse close to Joshua Tree. On our first trip there, I was first to use the outhouse. We had stopped for a late breakfast in a diner near a Marine base. Most of the customers were shaved-headed bottlenecks from the base, and though I felt uneasy in our beards—a sure sign that we were anti-war—the blueberry pancakes were huge. Unlike Ellie's carefully counted and apportioned blueberry pancakes, these were gigantic with fistfuls of blueberries thrown in. Sausage on the side? Of course. The coffee was strong.

Relieved to spot the outhouse, Terry graciously gave me toilet roll and I thankfully relieved myself with gusto. Handing the toilet roll to Terry, he followed suit. Reappearing a few minutes later, he asked laconically, "Er, Irwin, have you ever seen a black widow spider?"

I responded, "No, why?"

"Well, there was one sharing the seat with you when you were in the crapper. They like outhouses. It's always a good idea to check for them before you sit. They have this tell-tale red spot on their back."

"Thanks, Terry, I'll remember that."

Once I helped him waterproof the roof of his shack with tar and tarpaper. The temperature was well over a hundred degrees. When we finished, we stopped at a Chinese restaurant. I don't remember what we ate but it had to be better than Leo Ping's since the waitress was at least Chinese. What I remember most about the meal was the water. Terry had no running water in his shack, and we were surviving on chartreuse Gatorade.

When the waitress brought a jug of ice water we eagerly seized on and emptied it. With each table pass we asked for another pitcher. We each much have consumed several quarts of water. When we paid the tab the waitress said, "Wow, you guys were thirsty."

We shared many meals together. Like other Midwesterners I came to know, Terry was basically a carnivore and liked his meat well-done. He also would heavily salt things before he even tasted them. I learned this in a steak joint when he heavily salted *my* nostalgically ordered rare New York Strip sirloin before we realized it and I took his unsalted, but well-done steak. He sent mine back to be charred to death. I was left thinking about the German filmmaker Werner Herzog eating his own desert boot on film in front of an audience to honor a lost bet to Klaus Kinski.

Choosing a dish to share with Terry in a Chinese restaurant was also a challenge. Once, when I suggested a shrimp dish, he shuddered, saying that he ate "nothing below fish on the phylogenetic tree." What? That discussion went no further.

But perhaps the most meaningful personal discussion I ever had with anyone was when we went camping in Zion National Park. New Yorkers are not campers, at least not this one. Terry loved camping and he was the best person in the world to do it with. He knew about geology, about plants, about insects, about animals, and he shared his knowledge easily, non-pedantically and with youthful enthusiasm.

After a long day hiking, we settled in our campsite, put together a makeshift dinner, smoked some dope, and settled in our sleeping bags under an endlessly shimmering star-field sky. That's when we decided to finish the tequila bottle Terry had brought along. Passing the bottle back and forth, we talked about deep regrets as well as fervent hopes. Then Terry asked me a question the answer to which I've never forgotten. He asked me what my life's purpose was. Without hesitation I answered, "To love and be loved."

When I asked Terry, his answer came equally easily. "To know everything there is to know." What I said in that moment of tequila *veritas* and total transparency is a compass I follow to this day.

My only mistake that night was toasting our absolute love for each other with a cold can of Pepsi. If one can remember passing out, I belched and passed out. I remember the belch. It was heard all over Zion. The next morning, I awoke with a biblical hangover to the sound of four German tourists in the next campsite playing Telemann on recorders at 7:30 a.m. They had finished their breakfasts, completed their cacophonous cleanup by seven, and were now welcoming the new day and everyone else camping in Zion. Though I still like Telemann and do not hate all Germans, I've never touched a drop of tequila or Pepsi since. No great loss. But I am so, *so* grateful for that night I spent with Terry under the stars.

Terry never learned everything there is to know. He lifted weights and was the only non-physician I ever knew who owned his own stethoscope. I never asked why and assumed it was just another thing to know about. He married and had a son, whom he referred to as "the boy." I only met his wife and son briefly once on a trip to New York, but I remember thinking how lucky the boy was. Terry spent his career as a warden of the court, looking after the interests of mentally ill persons who lived in places like Terry had when he was evading the draft.

I hooked Terry up with a colleague of mine named Dan with whom I consulted at Mount Sinai Hospital. To my surprise, I learned that Dan loved climbing in Joshua Tree. Though from entirely different places, the Bronx and Detroit, they climbed rock faces together in Joshua Tree for years. It tickled me that they knew each other, though I admit to being slightly jealous of Dan. Still, I'm afraid of heights, and just watching climbers without safety ropes is impossible for me.

When Terry wasn't even yet sixty, Dan informed me that Terry had died of a heart attack after a round of golf. I couldn't imagine Terry playing golf. It seems so dorky and suburban. But I imagine that all that salt killed him, and carrying around his stethoscope only aided in his denial. Dan had learned this from a woman artist Terry had known who lived in the desert. Later she wrote to me to say that he had spoken of me often to her. There's so much I didn't know about Terry.

On learning of Terry's death, my first thought was about his son and the brilliant father and teacher he lost.

CHAPTER 6

EDWARD AND THE BALLAD OF
BOB'S BEEF BUFFET

B OB'S BEEF BUFFET was never a vegan hangout. Born on the highly overstated West Chicago Boulevard of Tecumseh, Michigan in 1974, it lived only until 1987. That was long before the vegan hordes descended. They didn't shut it down or drive it out with placards, protests, and screeds about sustainability. It probably just died of natural causes—gentrification and rent increases. It's remotely possible but unlikely, however, that my last visit to it was responsible for its decline.

As far as I knew, Bob's was the only restaurant in *downtown* Tecumseh. But that depends on what you call a restaurant. To a taxonomist of eating establishments, characterizing it presented a serious challenge. Sit-down restaurant, buffet, or cafeteria? It was all three.

Unlike newer places that offer "farm-to-table" menus, Bob's was a place where farmers came-to-table. Sometimes they brought their wives if one or another had a medical or dental appointment in town. Local gaggles of women might gather there in clusters of three or four to celebrate a birthday and/ or gossip. Other regulars were local firemen, police, clothing salesmen, and the occasional but rare New Yorker—me.

In the 1980s, I was a social work research consultant at Boysville of Michigan, a residential care facility for delinquent, predominantly Detroit boys. They had been placed there by the juvenile court in rural Clinton to remove them from bad influences and transplant them to barracks euphemistically called *cottages* where they could attend classes with other boys like themselves and breathe the clean country air while marching two-by-two from cottage to school and back. Though the boys were predominantly Black and Protestant, they attended Catholic Church services on Sundays. God is God everywhere, but Clinton is far from Detroit. And that was the point.

Later, whenever friends queried me about Boysville, I'd explain, "It was like the 1938 film, *Boys Town*, only in Clinton, Michigan." That was sufficient to end that line of enquiry.

But where is Clinton? Imagine I'm holding up my left hand and pointing to the center of my palm with my right index finger. Everyone's left hand is the shape of Lower Michigan. Lower Michiganders frequently use this device to locate their hometowns to non-Michiganders in winter while sitting around the pools at their Mexican timeshares. If they live in Michigan's Upper Peninsula, they have a problem. There's no way to capture both Upper and Lower Michigan's shape with one hand. But who would even bother? To Manhattanites, Michigan is just someplace else—except during presidential election years.

Those Manhattanites, local Zabarians and speakers of Yiddish, consider Michigan *dorten*—meaning something like "yonder" but closer to "over there, but who cares?"

They'd ask me, "What did I do *dorten*?" As succinctly as I could, I'd said, "I trained Holy Cross Brothers, Sisters of Mercy, and other Boysville staff to do program evaluation research."

Showing no interest at all in that, they'd ask where and with whom I ate lunch. "At Boysville? With delinquents? With gangbangers? With priests and nuns?" Not sure which was more frightening, I'd simply say, "At Bob's Beef Buffet with my buddy, Edward."

Edward was one of my dearest Michigan friends, and not only because he introduced me to Bob's. A former Holy Cross brother and Boysville executive director, he left the order to marry a former Holy Cross sister. Consequently, he was obliged to become Boysville's associate director. Step down or step up? To me it seemed like a double promotion. Though remaining devout Roman Catholics, in Boysville agency jargon, Edward and his wife were no longer labelled *religious*. That term was reserved for brothers and sisters who had taken vows of poverty and celibacy. Whether religious or not, the other Boysville staff with whom I worked were also not considered officially religious.

Like ladies who lunch at the Carlyle, when I was in Michigan, Edward and I lunched at Bob's.

We always entered from a no-charge, sparsely populated, not-attended parking lot. Because there was no signage to speak of, in rapt conversation over non-spiritual matters involving the Detroit Tigers or the New York Mets, Edward and I occasionally found ourselves in the men's clothing store next door to Bob's. Encountering all the shiny polyester, cellophane-wrapped shirts and racks of ties was always a shock—especially the garish ties. Well beyond my range, though my father and Edward might have chosen a few.

After a slight course correction, Edward and I would step outside and enter Bob's back door. Greeting us on the left was a slightly scary, oil portrait of a chef-in-toque—presumably Bob. On the right were hooks for hats and coats that you were never fearful of not finding on return. Unencumbered by winter gear for eight to ten months of the year, you would push forward, get in line; take an orange tray, paper napkin, silverware, glass of water; and slide yourself along a track in anticipation of an array of uninteresting choices, beginning of course with dessert. Various pies, cakes, and Jell-Os were among the sweet contenders. After desserts, salads of startling uniformity followed with a choice of the Holy Trinity of Midwestern salad dressings—French, Russian, or Thousand Island. (University of Michigan archaeologists hypothesized that though Tecumseh was landlocked, and ages ago there had been an iceberg in the area. How else to explain that no other kind of lettuce was known to exist in Bob's?)

After the salads, the food adventure really began. This is where the ubiquitous beef appeared. Steam trays with all sorts of beefy Midwestern treats beckoned customers and fogged my glasses. An overdone side of roast beef to be carved to order for *au jus* dipping. Beef burgers with any toppings you might request other than *foie gras.* Pure beef bologna just waiting to be grilled with an egg or without. Sunnyside, easy-over, or yolk broken? Corned beef, kraut, and Swiss for Reubens. A cauldron of chunky beef chili. A vat of barbecued beef of a color known only to Monsanto. Beef noodle soup or, for vegetarians, navy bean with your own sprinkle of phony bacon bits.

Ecumenical in his tastes, Edward always went for the chili and the navy bean. Though I loved him, the combination of the two made sitting next to him at afternoon meetings particularly resonant and risky from an olfactory POV. As for me, I couldn't resist the barbecued beef, wondering if I would glow in the dark when I returned to the Campus Inn, my hotel in Ann Arbor that night, sharing my bed with a local heartburn.

Behind the counter stood only the ever-genial Bob, wearing a chef's hat but looking nothing at all like the painting on the back wall. Still, there was always his welcoming smile, alternately taking orders while turning to flip and press burgers or puncture yolks on the flat-top behind. Once main courses were identified, executed, and handed over the glass counter, you could take a roll and pat of butter if you wanted to. Edward would always take several packs of saltines to break into his soup *and* his chili. That task completed, we would slide our trays to the beverage section, get our diet or regular Coke or A&W from a spigot, or avail ourselves of what was promised to be an *endless* cup of coffee or tea, however long the teabag lasted.

At the end of the tray-track rigidly sat a very stern-looking American Gothic-type woman (decidedly not goth) who would closely examine the contents of our trays and tell us that she'd have to charge extra for the second pat of butter or extra saltines. (Edward didn't care.) Then she'd rapidly tally our entire meal's cost peremptorily on the keys of her register, like a concert pianist ending a challenging concerto with a triumphant flourish. Neither Edward nor I would dare question her summation. Edward would signal with a circular wave that we were together, and she should put both trays on his tab. She never faulted in her encore. Rarely more than $13.50 for both of us, Edward's generosity of friendship always pleased me.

Once Edward paid, very polite and primly uniformed high-school-aged girls would carry our trays to the table of our choice. Putting food to table, they'd smile and say, "Thank you, sir," and, "Enjoy your lunch," then simultaneously remove our trays like synchronized swimmers after a perfect entry.

Now here's the funny part. On our first visit, Edward told me that Bob's was owned and run by identical twins. Obviously only one was Bob, but Edward didn't know the name of the other. He went on to explain that each worked the counter and grill on alternate days, but we never knew who was there on our day. So, to make things simpler we decided that both should be called Bob.

Aware of the absurdity of the situation, when I was not at Boysville but in New York or DC, our work-related, interstate telephone conversations often went somewhat like this:

Me: "Edward, have you been to Bob's lately? And how's Bob?"

Edward: "Bob is tip-top, but Bob is looking a bit run down." Or alternatively, "Bob has the flu, so Bob is standing in for him, working consecutive days."

Me: "Oh thanks. I hope Bob feels better soon, that must be rough on Bob. He's a really good guy."

Ed had a gruff voice and a hearty laugh that always ended with a deep and raucous cough. He was a heavy man and a heavy smoker. He was also a tender-hearted man who regularly sent get-well cards and inspirational poems he'd written to Fran when she was having her bone-marrow transplant.

But whatever my mood or worries at home, my fave at Bob's remained the barbecued beef on a bun. Just the right balance of sweet and spicy. $1.75 as I recall. The problem, however, was the bun. The oversized hamburger bun on which the soupy beef was ladled always fell apart while I was eating. This required picking up stray pieces of beef with my fingers and then matching them as best as I could to already soggy and malformed pieces of bun. In short, it was a mess. I was nearly a mess. Even more likely a disaster if I was wearing a tie or white shirt, though never from the store next door. Polyester would have protected me, but I preferred silk and cotton and had meetings to run back at Boysville after lunch. Nonetheless, I often returned to New York with questionable stains on my ties and shirts that no amount of French dry cleaning or Chinese hand laundering could erase. Edward's polyester ties were never threatened by his navy bean because he would always throw it over his shoulder before tucking in.

One day, while waiting my turn, I noticed the long "Crusty French" roll Bob dedicated to cradling mounds of roast beef for dipping into its purpose-sized *au jus* ramekin. Roll and ramekin fit perfectly together like—well, you know. Observing other diners, I realized that no matter how much dipping took place, the roll never fell apart. Yes, the ramekin occasionally overflowed, but the French roll held like Lafayette at Valley Forge.

In the moment surfaced my most brilliant Boysville consulting idea. With the *chutzpah* only a born-and-raised New Yorker is capable of summoning, I asked Bob whether I could have my customary barbecued beef on a French roll?

Bob, who happened to be behind the counter that day,

stepped back. I could see him eyeing his buns and rolls and inwardly counting how many of each he had left for roasted and barbecued beef remaining that day. After what seemed like a full minute of wondering about the wisdom of breaking tradition, his head snapped back as though awakening from a dream. Bob gave a quick affirmative nod and slathered my traditional barbecue on my nouveau crusty roll. Seeing this, the woman at the cashier seemed startled and confused. When I arrived at her station, she threw a questioning look at Bob. He just smiled and nodded, indicating apparently that it was okay, and she should just charge the usual price. She sighed audibly, probably thinking, *What is this city slicker trying to pull?* Reluctantly, she rang it up. Edward as usual paid and lunch was *que* perfection.

For my remaining five years at Boysville that was my standard lunch order at Bob's. When either Bob or Bob served me, all I needed to do was nod and whichever he was he'd smile as though we were both in on some very sophisticated cosmopolitan conspiracy.

Edward often came to New York to visit Fran and me and go to the theater. We'd always have dinner together at Il Mulino in Greenwich Village, but when he was on his own it would be Rosie O'Grady's across the street from his Midtown hotel. One of my happiest memories of Edward was taking him to the DXL Men's Big and Tall Apparel when he decided he needed a new wardrobe. He always wore dark suits, but they were left from his days as a *religious* and were shiny and worn. He had lost a few pounds for the occasion but was still rotund. But at DXL, compared to the other customers, he was as svelte as Fred Astaire. What I enjoyed most was watching the attractive middle-aged saleswoman—also of a certain size—flirting with him. He walked out with three suits, one of which he wore at his funeral, which I flew to New York to attend. The drone of the bagpipes broke my heart.

On my final day consulting at Boysville, four non-religious staff members took me to lunch at Bob's. By then, Edward had already passed. Which prefigured a sad, sweet-and-spicy farewell lunch. I ordered my usual. *Mais, apres moi, le deluge.* One after the other, each of my Boysville colleagues ordered barbecued beef on French rolls.

Somehow understanding the solemnity and significance of the moment, Bob didn't bat an eye. He knew that something special was happening. As did the cashier. She rang them up all together with a receipt handed to the last person in our party.

Behind us, while all this was happening, an elderly farmer in bib overalls and a double hearing aid turned to his wife in her flowered housedress and shouted loud enough for the whole place to hear, "What the hell is going on here?"

I was tempted to say, "Ask Bob," but didn't.

———————◇∞◇———————

Years later, after writing my original version of this story, I emailed it to my friend Paul who worked at Boysville at the time I did and once lived in Tecumseh. He loved Edward as well and knew him since he was religious.

Responding, he said he regretted telling me that the place was never called Bob's—it was Don's Beef Buffet—but what I'd said about the gentrification of Tecumseh was historically correct. In the '80s, property values skyrocketed, downtown businesses were forced to close, farms were sold and subdivided by developers. New and trendy restaurants proliferated. Local farmers who remained and didn't sell referred to the invading hordes simply as "them."

Frantically, I went back to Google and discovered that Paul was right. A tourist-targeted Tecumseh restaurant entry posted in 1986 invited a review of Don's. I was tempted but didn't. A real estate ad for a vacant space on 111 W. Chicago Boulevard posted in 1987 said that in its final year, Don's had fifteen employees and grossed $167,000. I now have in my possession the only remaining matchbook cover from Don's, which I purchased online for $3.50 plus shipping from MatchbookAlbum.com. The cover boasts "U.S. Prime Roast Beef Our Specialty." I don't miss Don's, which for me never existed, but I do miss Bob's. Far more, I miss Edward.

CHAPTER 7

BOGART AND BOVAIN, LIVING CLOSETED OR LIVIN' GOOD?

B OVAIN AND BOGART both hailed from the Deep South.
Both were Black men. That may be where the similarities
ended. But while Bovain called himself Bo, Bogart just called
himself Bogart. I loved them both.

Bogart was a PhD student of mine in Ann Arbor who became
my dean in New York City decades later. He was tall and thin,
moved gracefully, and dressed impeccably. He claimed to be an
excellent softball player. In the eyes of some, "effeminate", I could
easily imagine him gracefully chasing and gloving a fly ball in
centerfield, but he never played in our mixed student and faculty
softball games on Sundays. For all I knew he might have been in
church. He was very proud that his mother marched in Selma
and his primary research and policy interest was child welfare.
Though secretive about his personal life, his style could be
flamboyantly funny, falling to his knees and praying that I would
give him an extension on an overdue paper or bowing deeply to
Professor Epstein when he entered my office. To me, and later to
Fran, he was a Southern charmer and something of a puzzle.

After he completed his PhD, he took a teaching position and
later became an assistant then associate dean at Howard, the
historically Black university in Washington, DC. It suited him
and he did well there. That was the late '70s and we reconnected
when I did a sabbatical there in 1985 after Kayla and I split.

As a White Jewish man from New York City, that sabbatical
at Howard was for me equally educational, enlightening,

and extremely challenging. I saw how much more at ease Black graduate students were in exchanging ideas and taking intellectual risks, but I also experienced a kind of closing of ranks against me by students and faculty on occasions that was both understandable and hurtful. Together with an Asian Indian woman faculty member, I designed one of the first master's degree programs focused on working with displaced populations but was disturbed when many faculty objected to a program accepting White former Peace Corp members and Vietnamese physicians and lawyers who came here as *boat people* without the credentials to practice medicine or law in this country. To me, natural disasters and political oppression were equal opportunity tragedies but to many Howard Faculty their primary mission was to function primarily as Historically Black College and University (HBCU) serving Black students.

Another time I organized a Friday noon talk by a high-level officer of the National Institute of Mental Health, eager to encourage Howard faculty to submit research grants, but no one showed. After waiting half an hour, I apologized to my White guest, left and caught the next flight to Detroit for meetings at Boysville. When I returned from Detroit the following Monday, the dean chastised me, saying that the faculty claimed it was disrespectful of me to have left when I did. I needed to understand about "CPT," i.e., colored people's time.

I loved DC, but Howard didn't love me. I had a couple of romances that didn't last. I shared a room rather than an office with a Black part-time lecturer who lived near me in Adams-Morgan. Passing him having a smoke in front of our local 7-Eleven one night just before I returned to NYC, he stopped me to offer some final words: "Epstein, I used to think the worst thing in the world was being the only Black person teaching in an all-White school, but with all the shit that's been going down while you were here, I've had to change my opinion."

I hugged him and said, "That's the nicest thing anyone has said to me all year." He hugged me back. It wasn't tobacco he was smoking.

———————◇———————

I met Bo under entirely different circumstances. For years Fran had shared summer rentals with a racially diverse group of friends on Fire Island, which felt something like finding sabbatical homes for me and my kids every year in Ann Arbor. But we we found places in various Fire Island communities.

In addition to being our informal official driver, Bo was the official driver for a high-ranking New York City politician. But that was just one of many things he could do. A cook in the service, his stuffed zucchini blossoms and grits with pig parts were the stuff of legends. My only gripe with Bo's cooking was that he cooked like he drove—with his pot or his foot heavy on the gas. I loved his inventive meals, but I hated cleaning up after him on hot summer nights with a full stomach. By then, Bo was high and listening to music. But before every meal began, sitting at the head of the table wherever we were, he'd survey the meal he and the rest of us prepared and say, "We livin' good!" And we all agreed.

Bo was the only one who ever called me *homey*. I have no idea why he did, but I was always happy when he called to me from behind his and Tobi's bedroom door. "Homey, want to get intelligent with me?" Roughly translated, "Irwin, would you care to share some Mary Jane with me and confer about the state of the world?" Those confabs were better than any social work conferences I ever attended. There was always a soundtrack. Bo was partial to steel drum and island music, but there could be cool jazz or blues. He drank high octane rum that was smuggled in from the Caribbean and never wanted for Ganja. Summers, Bo and his steel band would have a three-week gig performing on an overnight ferry from Sweden to Finland and back. It was just something he did and returned exhausted with no stories to tell. I'm sure there were some, but he kept them to himself. Women loved him. Men too.

Once he told me that he was at his best "between two women." He didn't mean it in the three-way sense, but in relationship. So, while I was most aware of his very committed relationship with Tobi, I was vaguely aware of another woman somewhere in the background to whom he was devoted and would disappear occasionally to drive her to appointments for bee-sting injections to treat her MS. This was never a problem that I was aware of until Bo had his first heart attack and both women showed up at the same time to visit him at St. Luke's Hospital. I don't know the details, but I understood there was quite a ruckus. Despite his compromised health, most likely his formidable diplomatic skills were still available, and things settled down.

Under the influence of pot and alcohol, he and I solved many of the world's problems, from local to international, behind closed doors in his bedroom of whatever house we all shared on Fire Island. Gender, race, social class, you name it. Bo was his own man, and no matter what the social, political, or navigational dilemma, he was firmly and confidently in charge. He was all there. Solid. Fully present.

———◦⊃⊂◦———

Bogart was another story entirely. Out of a safe and comfortable social environment where he could be charming and quite witty, Bogart appeared frail, shy, and insecure. He might not show it. He might appear very smooth. But scratch the surface and he'd either run for cover or explode.

Though I supported his career move from Howard to Hunter, it was a dreadful mistake. No matter how glamorous it might

have seemed to him at the time, New York City and Hunter wer
not a good fit, and though the faculty were briefly charmed by
him, they quickly turned against him. And his responses to their
responses made things worse.

From the start, I worried about his diet and physical health.
Rail thin, I have sound evidence to believe that he lived almost
largely on take-out from KFC. He and I occasionally lunched in
his office and shared a tuna salad sandwich at my insistence. He
would eye it as though it was somewhat dangerous. For reasons
unknown, he would have it with a Diet Coke, which I would not
share. In a no-smoking building he began smoking cigarettes,
exhaling smoke out the window, the frequency of which seemed
to be correlated with his increasingly ineffectual performance in
his role as dean.

At the beginning of his tenure, and with an eye to promoting
new collaborations between our school and a medical center,
I arranged a lunch for him, myself, the director of social work
services, and a vice president for human resources at Mount
Sinai, where I was an adjunct professor and research consultant.
As it happened, that day Rabbi Menachem Schneerson, the
much-revered leader of the Lubervitcher Hassidic community
whom some believed was the Messiah, had been hospitalized
with a heart attack. From the restaurant window we could see the
streets around Mount Sinai filled with orthodox Jews bending
and unbending (a.k.a. *shuckling*) in prayer for their leader's
recovery.

Bogart, a gentle Southern fish in rough Northern waters, asked
me if this was some kind of protest. I explained that it wasn't. The
director of social work services, known for her timidity, worried
aloud, "What if Rabbi Schneerson dies and all the orthodox in
New York City blame Mount Sinai and never come here again for
services?" Known for his ever-present entrepreneurialism, the vice
president for human resources said, "Nonsense, we'll build him a

shrine and they'll flock to the hospital!"

Bogart didn't have a clue and didn't ask one question. He demonstrated no interest. He remained passive when he needed to be active.

I invited Bogart to join the National Research Advisory Committee I chaired at Boysville because of his wide knowledge of foster care systems and Black culture. There, Edward took a liking to him and when he came to town, the four of us—Fran, Bogart, Edward, and me—would have dinner and go to the theater. I suspect but don't know that those might have been the only occasions while living in New York that he went to the theater. When he wasn't at work, I wondered whether all he did was watch TV in his flash UES apartment building. I was never invited to his apartment and respected his desire for privacy.

Bogart was dean for a few years, but the faculty grew restive. He seemed depressed, smoked more, and became edgy. You couldn't miss the smell of smoke in his office. Though active in national professional organization activities outside the school, he became less and less engaged and even present inside the school. I felt concerned and protective. He was a very sweet and charming guy, but now clearly over his head in waters filled with circling sharks. I cared deeply for him but could not do for him what he needed to do for himself and for his school.

In his early fifties, he began talking about early retirement, returning to his ancestral home in Alabama, just to sit in his porch, manage a few family properties, and maybe start an antique business. The university was offering early retirement packages for administrators with relatively high salaries to cut costs, looking for those who'd had enough of City University budget cuts. Bogart had had enough of Hunter faculty.

That August, I received a request from the president of the college to meet with her. That was highly unusual, and I thought she might have a special assignment for me and was excited about the possibility. How right I was about the special assignment and how wrong I was to be excited.

In our meeting she began by saying that she was aware that Bogart and I were good friends. Not knowing where this was going, I acknowledged that it was true. Then she informed me that over the summer a group of very influential senior faculty had met with her to complain about Bogart's performance as dean, and she had received similar complaints from outside school benefactors. Though the complaints were probably justified, I said nothing.

I was there because she wanted Bogart to announce his forthcoming retirement at the opening of the new school year in our first faculty meeting. After that, she would hire a highly skilled academic search firm to initiate a search for a new dean. As an aside, she reminded me to remind Bogart that she was a lawyer, had worked in the Giuliani administration, and it would be a great mistake if Bogart decided to play the race card.

On the other hand, if he agreed, she'd be happy to extend his salary for a year and send him to Harvard Business School if he wanted to become a dean elsewhere, or provide an office if he decided to write a book. But she made it clear, she wanted him out—and she wanted me to tell him.

I told her that I didn't think that was my job, but as his friend I would help him decide what he wanted to do and negotiate his exit package. We agreed to that.

Though I had a scheduled meeting at Mount Sinai later that afternoon, I stopped in his office and asked how long he would be there. Without telling him anything about my meeting with the president, I knew he would do far better financially and professionally if he negotiated a settlement rather than taking the standard and not-very-generous early retirement package that the university was offering everyone else.

Later, I asked him whether he'd like to go out for a drink,

realizing that I'd never had a drink alone with him even though we'd been through every combination of academic ranks over thirty years at three universities. Bogart rejected the suggestion, opened his window, lit a cigarette, and quietly listened to what I had to tell him.

I was now the messenger, and it killed our friendship. After making some outlandish threats to hire Johnnie Cochran and sue both the university and the faculty who complained about him, he stopped talking to me. At our first faculty meeting he announced his retirement and "held the course" (his favorite expression) for the remainder of the year. He never returned my calls to his personal phone. We never said goodbye. There was no party for him. I was relieved about that.

About a year later, his secretary, Pat, the only person at Hunter with whom he'd maintained regular contact, told me that he'd had a stroke and died.

In the eighties, after the Fire-Island-house-share phase of our respective lives, Fran and I bought a little beach house in Ocean Grove, New Jersey. I'd had it with house shares. But Fran probably could have gone on.

She was always grateful to them for taking her and her ten-year-old, Molly, in to join their collective when Fran had been a divorced and single parent. Bo and Tobi instantly became kindly surrogate uncle and aunt to Molly. Years later when Molly successfully applied to Brown University, she wrote her application essay about them. Playing seven-card stud as they often did, including Molly, she learned from Bo to say, "Down and dirty like the old folks do," when the final closed card was dealt. Who knows? That card may have opened the door for her to Brown.

Whether in Fire Island or Ocean Grove, Bo never swam. I

suspect the Atlantic was too cold. But wherever they were, both he and Tobi loved surf-fishing together. They both fished avidly on vacation in Belize every winter. Maybe he swam there. I don't know. It never occurred to me to ask.

Their last day visiting us at Ocean Grove was extremely hot, but Tobi and Bo insisted on walking the seven blocks from our little house to the wide beach and across the hot sand to the ocean with their surf-casting poles and gear. Stripers were running. Bo loved catching, cleaning, and cooking fish. As with other things, he did all three expertly.

Crossing the wide stretch of sand, I noticed Bo was sweating profusely and having trouble breathing. Nonetheless, he insisted that he was fine. He came to fish and the stripers were running. But after a few minutes I asked him for his car keys, ran home, turned on his automobile air conditioner, and double-parked near the boardwalk. Then I convinced him to leave with me despite his resistance. Tobi stayed but caught nothing.

Later that year, Bo was found dead of a heart attack in his Harlem apartment filled with African masks, prints, and all sorts of memorabilia. But no drums. A year before, he had donated his *steel* collection to the Studio Museum of Harlem. Bo took care of business.

Fran and I accompanied Tobi to identify the body and wait for the coroner to arrive.

For practicality and convenience's sake, the viewing was held at an old Jewish funeral parlor on the Upper West Side of Manhattan. Both his women and other intimates who loved him were there and sat around and told homely stories about him.

Months later, the memorial service and celebration of his life was held at a posh modern art gallery in newly fashionable Chelsea. It was spectacular and joyous, filled with musicians and politicos, artists, writers, and very likely his ganja and rum supplier. The politician for whom he drove made a surprisingly eloquent and witty speech. Who knew he was so refined? Bo would have felt equally at home in each setting—a modest Jewish funeral home and a chichi art gallery. He fit in and found friends everywhere. As his "homey" I was at both, trying through my tears and laughter to look intelligent.

CHAPTER 8

ELLIE/ELI, WHAT'S IN A NAME? EVERYTHING

NOW, I THINK about another "Ellie"—not Clark's wife. Ellie was a PhD student of mine when she registered for my dissertation seminar in the fall of '09. A self-described "butch lesbian" in her late forties, Eleanor wore outrageously wide and garish men's ties (ties I would never wear) along with conventional and informal men's clothing (that I would). No Scottish tweed sports coats, but jeans and man-tailored shirts that fit awkwardly. I was convinced her dress combined a mockery of straight men with a wish to join them. She was never especially friendly to me, but I wasn't looking for friendship from my students. If it presented itself, I welcomed it. If not, I was a teacher and didn't need to be loved by individual students, though I enjoyed it when an entire class manifested their affection for me through their eagerness to learn.

Ellie was aloof when she first appeared in class—often late—and remained so well into the semester. We discussed her dissertation ideas desultorily. Nothing took flight.

By chance, Fran and I met Ellie and her wife and two dogs on a walk in Ocean Grove where Fran and I had bought our sweet, red, flat-roofed cottage in 2002. Ellie's wife, we discovered, ran a B&B in OG, and Ellie commuted to New York for work and political activism. They had adopted a bi-racial son years before. He was now a teenager.

Halfway through the semester, Ellie informed her classmates and me that she/he now wished to be called either Eli or Elihu and was embarking on a complete change of sex and gender.

For several years an LGBTQ activist and health services community organizer for gays, lesbians, and other marginalized groups, Eli informed me as well that he wanted to change his dissertation topic from telling the story of the battle for LGBTQ health services in Greenwich Village to telling the story of his own personal and multifaceted transition from butch lesbian to transman married to a woman with children. And what a complex, painful, and ultimately courageous story it was. I won't say *triumphant* for reasons that will become clear, though Eli did what Ellie had only wished he then she could do from childhood but thought impossible until his late forties.

As someone who was once accused of being a "dissertation romantic," I was always up for supporting students' scholarly and rigorous investigations of subjects they felt passionately about and had at least some implications for social work practice or policy. I'd guided former doctoral students at universities in Hong Kong, New York, Melbourne, and Washington through studies that spanned the life cycle on topics that ranged from *in-vitro* fertilization after unmourned miscarriages in the United States to *good death* among Hong Kong Chinese cancer patients. They were not all that heavy. I chaired a dissertation on the use of Nuyorican poetry as *biblio-therapy* with Puerto Rican adolescent boys. Another was about resolving interpersonal and professional conflicts among string quartet members. The key for me was whether the student was passionately invested in the topic and willing to pursue it systematically and in a scholarly manner.

Rather than a dissertation romantic, I think of myself as a *methodological pluralist*—someone who does not favor one or another research method but is open to all. For me, there is no gold standard of experimental research design for randomized clinical trials with *real doctors* at the apex, as most social work researchers believe. Instead, I believe that every method has its strengths and limitations. In fact, I have often sponsored dissertations that combine different methodological approaches. But if I'm known for anything among my academic research colleagues, it's for introducing and championing clinical data mining, which relies on retrieving and analyzing information that is routinely available but rarely used for knowledge generation. Some might disparagingly call it *dumpster-diving*, but I like to think of it as seriously cooking with leftovers—from the fridge, not the dumpster.

I've paid a price for my methodological unorthodoxy and have been regarded as something of a heretic in establishment American social work research circles; a hero in irreverent Australian research circles; a neo-liberal, post-positivist American hack in the UK; and an esteemed professor in Hong Kong. All fine with me, though I got treated best in Hong Kong— probably because of my age.

Nonetheless, Eli's research proposal represented a serious challenge for me and for my PhD program faculty colleagues. His chosen topic was no problem—the social and psychological barriers confronting individuals going through a sex change. The problem was that Eli wanted to write about himself.

Despite their variations and combinations, all my previous dissertation supervisions had employed relatively conventional research methods—both qualitative and/or quantitative. One involved comparative qualitative analysis of groups as small as five seeking reunification with their children currently in foster care. Another involved evaluation of a national public health and poverty program with a cast of thousands in Chile. My academic colleagues both at home and abroad accepted each as legitimate. As long as students followed established research protocols, no one cared about their personal reasons for choosing the topic. *My* only requirement was that in pursuing their topic, they could discover that they were wrong.

I recall a qualitative PhD dissertation conducted at the University of Michigan concerning single fathers—a topic with which I was quite familiar. The purpose of the study was to describe the lives of Ann Arbor single fathers who spent at least half of their time caring for or seeing to the care of their children. That described me one hundred percent of the time at that period of my life.

To do this, Harry, the student, conducted lengthy interviews with all those he could find in the area. There weren't many, but the interviews were in depth. His sparse literature review was as good as it could be, and his interview guide was comprehensive. But when he started giving me findings chapters, I had the sense that there was something very wrong. All his respondents seemed to be saying how great it was to be a single dad—that they had more women friends, had learned to do all sorts of childcare and household tasks, felt more emotionally open and sensitive, and their kids provided all manner of joys and gratifications.

Wait a minute, Harry, I thought but did not say, *this sounds nothing like my life,* a comment that stuck in my own craw since my dissertation defense. Mine was a study of close to nine hundred social workers and their political attitudes and actions. An outside member of my committee said that my findings were nothing like his social worker aunt's attitudes and actions.

Here I was thinking something similarly epistemologically inappropriate. Instead, I commented, "Harry, it strikes me that most of these guys are sharing childcare with their exes. Aren't any of them complaining about the burdens of being a single parent—male or female?" "Oh," Harry responded. "I only wanted to say what was good about men expanding their role-repertoires."

Upon additional analysis, it became clear that while these men had more women friends, the number of male friends they'd had dropped precipitously, and several had been forced to give up full-time jobs they'd liked or graduate degrees they were pursuing. Compared to them, I had it really good, but Harry's findings and conclusions needed to be balanced to comport with his data and fit reality, not with his cherry-picked data to bake in his ideological pie.

Eli's problem was different. He proposed telling his story with a newly emerging methodology called *auto-ethnography*—a qualitative study approach in which the object of study is the author herself or himself. It's the opposite of what some call autobiographical fiction. It's autobiographical truth as scholarship.

In response to my efforts to gather the required three other faculty members, I first approached the person who mainly taught qualitative methods on our PhD faculty. He stormed out of my office when I described the project to him, huffing and puffing that, "It's impossible for someone to study oneself and write about oneself objectively." *But I thought qualitative methods were about scholarly and disciplined subjectivity?*

Other less exclusively qualitative-methods-oriented faculty demurred because the first professor I approached who was so vehemently opposed was also chair of the PhD program and known for his doctrinaire positions on almost everything. Ultimately, I cobbled together a necessary and sufficiently solid committee of four—myself as chair, a somewhat junior lesbian activist member of the faculty, and a straight woman and senior professor who was an established expert on adolescent sexual development. Eli found someone whose presentation on auto-ethnography he had attended at a recent professional conference. He was from a Catholic University in Washington, DC, and attended all our meetings as well as the dissertation defense via Zoom.

Borrowing from Irving Goffman's brilliant theoretical classic entitled *The Presentation of Self in Everyday Life,* I reintroduced Eli to Goffman's writings on *Stigma,* none of which required data collection other than Goffman's keen perceptions of people and institutions. Accordingly, I suggested that Eli entitle the dissertation, "The Presentation of 'Trans' in Everyday Life" because that's exactly what it was all about.

Beginning with his childhood in a strict Methodist home, refusing to wear a dress and insisting he was a boy, Eli described all manner of Goffmanesque social nightmares and contradictions that faced him in his present life—for example, keeping a scheduled appointment with a gynecologist when he had already grown a beard and being told by the receptionist that, "There must be some mistake," and having to show identification. Bathroom altercations. Career challenges as he changed physically in the classes he was teaching at Columbia or for the patients he was seeing in his psychotherapy private practice.

All seemed to be going well, until his dissertation defense. Unfortunately, in American doctoral programs, *defense* is a perfect description. Prove to us that you are worthy of the doctoral degree. In the UK, it is referred to as a *viva voce* in which students give *living voice* to their work. I find that concept much more congenial, collegial, and consistent with my philosophy of education.

In our program, it was common practice for committee members to alert the chair if they felt there was something fundamentally wrong with the dissertation so that a defense would not be scheduled until the problems were substantially addressed. Eli was pushing for the defense because a full-time, entry-level job was offered him at Columbia University School of Social Work contingent upon his having a degree in hand by June of that year.

This hiring practice was not common in my day because many entry-level positions in social work didn't require a doctorate. In my case, my *future* credential profile was already considered so impressive (a PhD from Columbia in Sociology) that I was treated like a bonus baby in baseball before I'd completed my dissertation. Schools were competing for me. And once I accepted the position at Michigan, I received an unrequested bump in salary in lieu of moving expenses *plus* a reduced teaching load to encourage me to finish my degree and begin publishing ASAP.

Today, there are lots of PhDs on the job market, many already with peer-reviewed professional publications. Prestigious research universities are now seeking candidates who have completed post-doctoral programs.

For Eli, there was a lot at stake in completing his PhD by the end of that spring semester. Schools were no longer accepting promises from applicants that they would be finished—nor would they accept letters from the doctoral advisors to that effect. The game had changed. But Eli had weathered his stormy years of surgery and recovery and done so well in part-time teaching at Columbia that they had offered him a full-time job on a tenure-bearing line. That was as good as it gets from Columbia. But that hiring condition was non-negotiable. Everyone on his committee knew it.

Unfortunately, his doctoral defense gradually spiraled from a cordial conversation into a round of questions which became increasingly contentious between two faculty members who were established experts on childhood and adolescent sexual development on the one hand and feminism on the other. No one questioned the legitimacy of auto-ethnography and, in fact, the outside expert on the subject was quite pleased with the study and its execution.

Finally, the moment came when the candidate is asked to leave the room so the committee can deliberate. As chair, I was responsible for achieving a consensus and sign-off by all faculty participants. On the form that our university used, there were four categories: (1) Pass as presented, with only typos and misspellings corrected; (2) Pass with Minor Substantive Corrections, which only the chair must approve; (3) Pass with Major Substantive Corrections, which require a reconvening of the original committee and a new defense; and (4) Fail. In a half century of dissertation advising to countless DSWs and PhDs in several countries, no one had ever failed on my watch. Not because standards were low, I assure you. But because a failing work and undeserving student never made it as far as the defense.

Once on a trip with another American academic to the former Soviet Republics of Georgia and Kyrgyzstan, I interviewed several finalists for American PhD study-fellowships in social science and social work, sponsored by the Open Society Foundation. The trip offered several surprises—both personal, professional, and oenological. Georgians claim to have discovered wine-making. They have reason to be proud. Who knew?

Getting past customs in Georgia was slow (nothing new) but required some *baksheesh*. We then drove at 2 a.m. to our hotel in Georgia's capital, Tbilisi, in a snowstorm with a driver who smelled of *slivovitz,* the prune whisky my paternal grandfather consumed and used as aftershave. The windshield wipers wheezed while struggling to cut through heavy clumps. Turning off a very modern highway, I looked up at the road sign which said *Tbilisi*. Pure relief, no surprise. But in parenthesis under Tbilisi, slightly smaller but also in white against green, the sign said *Tiflis*—that was where my paternal grandfather was born! As a young man, hiding his Jewishness, he'd served in the Russo-Japanese War fighting as far from Tiflis as Vladivostok. Afterwards he married an exotic, Asian-eyed beauty, who also happened to be Jewish, and they found their way to a tenement in East Harlem where my father was born—an American citizen. I wasn't even in bed yet, but I'd already had a major dose of memory lane in the taxi.

Once in the shabby but still imperial hotel, my travel

partner and fellow judge, Gretchen, and I shared a terrific steak frites and a bottle of a fabulous Georgian red Saperavi—a very welcome surprise at 3 a.m. augmented later that week by traditional Georgian food and other wines. I learned there that Georgia is generally considered the cradle of winemaking dating back in the South Caucasus to 6,000 B.C.

Gretchen, my partner in wine-tasting, was an educationalist and qualitative researcher, and we got along marvelously. The next couple of days involved interviewing spectacular fellowship applicants who were teaching, working in non-profits, or conducting research in fields ranging from anthropology to social work and public health—all fluent in at least Georgian, Russian, and English and all eager to come to the United States to secure an American PhD in their chosen field.

After the glorious surprise of being in the presence of one after another glitteringly intelligent and eager applicant, it occurred to me that several already had PhDs. When asked why they would want another, the consensus seemed to be, "An American PhD means so much more." American academic chauvinism aside, over the course of the day, our questioning revealed that PhDs in Georgian Universities and others were still affected by the Russian system where they could be bought as well as worked for. No matter how bright the student, envelopes with money were expected by PhD advisors and mentors. And unlike the United States educational system, PhD students were not required to take coursework of any kind—simply conduct dissertation research under the guidance of their sponsor.

When candidates were asked about this practice, explanations offered ranged from, "University professors here get paid so little, they deserve it," to, "That's just the way it is." Several seemed embittered about it and one young woman applicant looked slightly tearful while she silently shrugged her shoulders. I asked her nothing more about it but wondered whether her Georgian PhD cost her more than euros.

Rank-ordering candidates for selection was extremely challenging but remarkably satisfying for Gretchen and me. Out of a possible twenty candidates we could only choose five. We did, and a Georgian academic and friend of an Armenian American former PhD student of mine took us to a local nightclub to celebrate completion of our complex task.

The room was smoky, a three-piece band was playing, and the food and wine were now as expected. Our choice table was close to the band and we three were the only ones speaking English in the room. A young woman sat on a stool with a hand mic singing Georgian songs that were not recognizable and American tunes in Georgian that were. Though Gretchen and I would have loved to stay, we needed to get up early to fly to Bishkek in Kyrgyzstan to do another two rounds of interviews. Though we resisted, our Georgian host picked up the tab. As we got up to leave, the piano player struck a few chords that were immediately recognizable and wonderfully familiar to me. He was playing the intro to "Take the 'A' Train" by Billy Strayhorn and Duke Ellington. In response to my recognition, the smile on his face said, "Farewell," rather than, "Get the hell out of here!"

Our interviews in Bishkek followed a similar path to Tbilisi. The food wasn't as good, and the roads and sidewalks were a mess. But ornate, newly constructed official buildings with gold-laminated statues of historical, military, and political heroes struck a surprising contrast to the claptrap infrastructure. I found a crafts shop where I bought a lovely boiled-wool winter hat for Fran. The store owners seemed shocked that a man would buy a hat for a woman. Fran still gets compliments and tries to remember *Kyrgyzstan* when people ask.

Though the applicants were more phenotypically and ethnically varied in their appearance than those in Georgia, stories about slipping envelopes to PhD advisors and the superiority of American PhDs were by now familiar to us.

Gretchen and I left for home from Bishkek on a very different note than we did on exiting Tbilisi. On our last night, Gretchen and I were taken to a very sleek, Russian-style nightclub/disco to celebrate by our local hosts. They picked up the tab, but we paid a price as well—food poisoning.

Returning from Bishkek to Manhattan, once the PhD candidate is asked to leave the room, if the outcome is easy to agree to and the candidate did a magnificent job, faculty might heighten the drama for the student by discussing summer vacation plans, an apartment they are purchasing, a restaurant they discovered, and the like. Then the candidate who has the highest box checked is congratulated, called *doctor,* and hands are shaken.

In instances in which the penultimate grade is received—Pass with Minor Corrections—congratulations and "doctor" are offered, the chair summarizes the closed-door discussion, and the candidate agrees to make the required changes under the supervision and sign-off by the chair alone.

Eli remained outside the committee room for close to a half-hour while those of us in the room discussed the dissertation—*not* our summer plans. Surprisingly, no one challenged his auto-ethnographic choice of research methodology. In fact, his outside expert seemed quite satisfied. However, my two local colleagues said they were extremely dissatisfied for two very different and possibly conflicting reasons. What they agreed on was, Pass, with Major Revisions. Major revisions requiring another formal defense and a sign-off by all committee members.

Why, I wondered, hadn't their concerns come up before the defense was scheduled? My strategy was to hear them out and suggest that we officially consider these minor revisions that I could sign off on but that they could informally approve before the deadline for getting his degree. In that way, Eli could graduate, take his teaching job at Columbia, and possibly publish his dissertation as a book. Instead, my two local colleagues each insisted on a major rewrite and another formal defense to be sure that he fully understood and incorporated their corrections. His written words were not enough.

What were they so adamant about? The expert on psycho-sexual development of children and adolescents took the position that Eli's account of his gender *dysmorphia* was theoretically impossible, that he was too young to claim it and it did not comport with her writing on the subject. The expert on feminism and all matters LGBTQ claimed that his concluding chapter about finally being experienced as a man by others as well as his nominally straight wife reeked of "male triumphalism and patriarchy."

Partially explaining this to Eli in the hallway outside the seminar room was like dropping the hammer on Bogart in his office—but this time facing the company of others. At first, he refused to enter the room. Again, I was the reluctant messenger. Red-faced and furious, he could barely listen to the reasons why he could not move on in his career to a coveted job at Columbia. The outside member Zooming in from Washington seemed disgusted and the TV with his image went blank. The others left and I tried to dissuade Eli from dropping out of the PhD program. That took weeks more.

Ultimately, he finished his PhD but lost his Columbia job. He found one in a less prestigious school requiring him and his new family to move to Connecticut. He published a book and at a reading at the Gay Men's Health Crisis, I met his Danish wife and his newly adopted children. He continued to do counseling with families in which children and adolescents wanted to transition to male or female. He met with friends of ours in Ocean Grove whose Charlotte is now Charlie. Two years after he received his degree and seemed happily placed in his new teaching position, I learned that he was diagnosed with pancreatic cancer. His wife posted daily in ethnographic detail about his progress on a site that solicited money for itself, and the families involved. I posted a note to him about his courage but received no response. Perhaps he was still angry with me. I couldn't read the daily reports because they were too much like Fran's daily reports—except Fran was doing well.

Eli was around fifty when he died, and I can't help thinking that his American PhD might have cost him a great deal more than his Georgian and Kyrgis female compeers.

CHAPTER 9

TONY T, COGNITIVE COMPLEXITY AND EMOTIONAL UNDERDEVELOPMENT

THERE WERE TWO Tonys in my life who played major roles in my career and relatively minor roles in my personal and inner life. Tony T intrigued me from the start when we met in a doctoral research design course that we both took in Columbia's School of Social Work in 1963. He was working on his doctorate in social work (DSW) focused on applied perceptual psychology. I was simultaneously working on my master's degree in social work and my PhD in sociology—all at Columbia. I found his research interests and their applications fascinating. But he never showed *any* interest in my field of sociology or its applications. I suspect he thought sociology was obvious, or bullshit, or not a science. Nonetheless, he seemed interested in me as a person.

Tony and I met and began eating lunch together between classes on a bench in the Carnegie Mansion's lush garden. The friendship lasted about half a century. Tall and darkly handsome, with velvety brown eyes and big dimples on his moon-shaped face, I didn't realize until later that he was a different kind of chick magnet than my MFY mentor, Richard. Instead, Tony had a kind of quiet understated macho charisma—less showy, but for some women even more compelling.

Italian American by birth, when we first met and he still smoked, he postured like one of the *ragazzi* in a film by Pasolini. Cupping his cigarette backwards in his right hand, he'd prop one foot against a wall, any wall. It didn't matter if he left a shoeprint. He probably enjoyed it if he did.

Years before pocket calculators, Tony brandished a slide-rule to do statistical calculations with the same bravado that a street-tough in Rome or Naples or Calabria, where his family was from, would display his switchblade. My dear friend Harold would have called him just another bad boy. But Tony tried very hard to be good and often acted like a Boy Scout despite his darker side. In today's jargon, Tony was a sexy nerd, a James Dean who could compute his own Chi-squares.

I was five years younger, and he was already married and had a daughter. I never knew why exactly he was interested in me. Maybe he was looking for a smart younger brother whom he could help make it in the world. Unfortunately, that generous impulse got terribly twisted and distorted where women were concerned.

Tony's doctoral research concerned *cognitive complexity*, a concept I found compelling but the study of which I found reductionist and simplistic. Not unlike Tony in many respects. It's akin to my caustic sociology co-chair, Sy, operationally defining human beings as "featherless bi-peds." For research purposes, CC was measured by how many background factors subjects considered in making decisions about artificially constructed vignettes. To me, even in my twenties, human complexity was far more complex than that. Tony proudly told me that he scored in the top of the top percentile of the population. No doubt he did.

To a practicing social worker or any kind of clinician, a high cognitive complexity score would predict greater diagnostic acuity based on the cues or symptoms offered by the prospective client or patient. To a homicide detective, a high score would translate to how many clues she might consider in naming the killer. If the measure had been around and he would have deigned to be tested, Sherlock Holmes would no doubt have been in the top of the top percentile along with Tony

T. However, it seems relevant to point out that, as Tony and I were having lunch together one day, I spied Basil Rathbone, who played Sherlock impeccably in so many British films, walking determinedly down 5th Avenue. Perhaps, I fancied, he was headed to the Metropolitan Museum and the Egyptian collection. Excitedly, I turned and remarked, "Tony, do you see who that is? It's Basil Rathbone!"

To which Tony replied, "Who's he?"

I didn't bother to explain.

I have no idea how I would have scored on Tony's measure and didn't ask to be tested. I just assumed he would have done better than me and left it at that. I had nothing to prove and admired his intuitive statistical skills, which I never possessed. Tony was something of a genius at statistics but never doubted how universally smart that meant he was. I did, but maybe he was ahead of his time. To those who think all knowledge can be reduced to zeroes and ones, he was. It's all on Wikipedia.

In casual conversation, through his smiling silences and the occasional wry remark, he let you know that he already knew whatever it was that you knew. Some would call it arrogance. But there was something genuinely boyish, warm, and likeable about him. Then again, there was something rigidly stubborn and closed off as well. Like a UXB demolitions sapper, he was never wrong until it was too late, and by then the damage had been done to others as well as to himself.

Tony thought himself deep and complex. Maybe he was. *But how complex could he be,* I wondered, *making the same sandwich for lunch for himself every day of his life—salami and cheese on dark bread, and afterwards an apple?* Still, he had a powerful linear intelligence that carried him from being a delinquent kid in Sacramento to a doctorate at Columbia University, several professorships here and abroad, and ultimately a number of deanships.

Tragically, Tony's mother had died in a mental hospital when he was quite young. He never spoke of his father, but did proudly of his uncle Torchi, who owned a large restaurant in Sacramento and my guess was connected to the mob. Tony always insisted however, that the Mafia was an anti-Italian prejudicial fiction. He cringed when I told him I loved watching *The Sopranos*.

⸺◯⸺

From what Tony told me, one of his high school teachers (probably a woman) saw something in him beyond his tough, know-it-all presentation of self. After high school, he started in a community college, transferred to university, played football, and excelled in biostatistics. How he found his way into social work school at UC Berkeley was always a mystery. I never asked. Maybe it was his mother's illness and his inability to help her? He did once reveal that as a little boy, a visit to her in the mental hospital and her hysterical screaming upon seeing him so traumatized him that he remained deathly afraid of hospitals for almost his entire life until the end.

Tony completed his doctorate a few years before I finished mine. He had a brief stay as an assistant professor on the faculty at Columbia where senior faculty humiliated him by asking him to tend bar at a faculty Christmas party. After that, he moved to his entry-level dream job at UC Berkeley. I was happy for him. I knew an assistant professorship leading to a career at Berkeley was his greatest aspiration at the time. To my surprise, only three years later, he left Berkeley for an associate professorship at the University of Michigan, where he recruited me to join him in 1968, even before I completed my PhD. By then, I was married and had a son.

For many reasons, including the prospect of our writing

together, Michigan was an ideal career move for me. By then, Tony had two children—a girl and a boy. He liked Michigan much more than I did, was an avid U of M football fan, and consciously paved the way for a successful career for me. Beyond that, we were colleagues joined together by ideas and the play of our very different intelligences. Possibly brothers under the skin. More like my brother than my brother.

However, what I learned when I got to Michigan was that Tony had left Berkeley partly because of woman trouble. Or was it a dual opportunity? He'd persuaded a student with whom he'd had an affair at Berkeley to leave her husband and follow him to Ann Arbor to pursue a PhD at Michigan. He'd explained it all to me as he always did by saying, "She's *really* smart." I made no comment. They published a paper together, though she later left him and remarried.

He seemed surprised and devastated by it. Not unexpectedly, a few years later his marriage fell apart. When he was getting a divorce, I helped him move out of his home while his children watched. It was a very sad scene, but we were friends. Friends in trouble help each other. Right?

During much of our friendship, I told myself that Tony was an incurable romantic. Over time, and very sadly, I came to think of him as a self-deluded sexual predator. He was always falling in love with the perfect *really smart* and not-coincidentally beautiful woman who eventually turned out to be terribly imperfect. Or she discovered he was. When ditched, he might pine for years. I never sympathized. But I listened.

At Michigan, Tony rose quickly to full professor. I might have risen faster, but I refused to advocate for an early promotion for myself. I thought it was all about my work and shouldn't have to justify it. He agreed, but the difference was our organizational politics and my identification with student activism. He became full three years after associate. It took me twice as long—a price

I was willing to pay for my brand of irreverence.

Just as my politics were an embarrassment to him, what I experienced as Tony's social boorishness was for much of our lives working together an embarrassment to me. At the *instructional* brunch Lyn and I served to U of M faculty and their spouses in reparation for all the overdone roast beef dinners we had consumed, you may remember that I served a Cajun shrimp and rice dish I cooked with gargantuan shrimp. The shrimp were purchased at a price a lowly assistant professor could barely afford on a salary of $11,200 *per annum*. Even in 1969, those monsters were a buck apiece. What would that be today?

Everyone else got the picture—they happily ate their shrimp and rice together. The fact that the shrimp were carefully arranged on top of the casserole was an aesthetic choice, not an invitation to stuff your face with shrimp. That cognitively complex decision of mine apparently eluded Tony's complexity. Or he chose to ignore it.

While others were scattered about our sunny Ann Arbor living room with plates on their knees and a chilled wine at their feet, I remember Tony lingering at the buffet table picking out shrimp and eating them one by one. I approached him gently, not wanting to offend someone who'd gotten me there, and said, "Tony. That's a shrimp *and* rice dish. You're supposed to eat the shrimp *with* the rice." Tony looked back at me, smiled that dimpled smile of his, and responded, "I just like the shrimp!"

Over the course of my career, Tony and I wrote several books and many more articles together. He was much more prolific than I and published with several other faculty colleagues and doctoral students.

He and I specialized in program evaluation research. In

addition, we each had followed diverse tracks in our writing. He wrote about innovations in research methodology, and I wrote about the politics of professionalization and the politics inherent in research and practice.

He was also far more conservative politically than I. Cynical about politics, my professed radicalism was probably an embarrassment to him. Ultimately, he aspired to be a dean. I'm not sure why. I never wanted to be a dean. If anything, I drove deans crazy with my advocacy for student involvement in decision-making. Like Tony and my Cajun shrimp, I just liked teaching students to think.

I don't know how much Tony liked teaching. I'm sure he was a meticulous reader of student papers and doctoral dissertations. I suspected that as a teacher he was probably intellectually acute and demanding but slightly boring, dismissive, and doctrinaire. He only liked the really smart ones—female and male—like me. Over the years, I attended a few of his guest lectures. They were always deeply thoughtful and intelligent, but his jokes were really bad, and he'd have to laugh at them himself. If I told one to him, he would repeat the punchline as though he thought of it. Only then, when it became *his,* would he laugh.

We each loved mentoring. His mentees more frequently than mine were beautiful women whom he described again as "really smart" and with whom he later offered to write articles and books. To me all the smart ones were beautiful. But also the not-so-smart who tried, really tried, despite their lack of intellectual, genetic, and social-class privilege. Maybe I was the true romantic?

The first paper Tony T and I published together was one about evaluating innovative social action programs in health settings. We wrote it in one day in his basement and it seemed so simplistic to me sociologically that I found it an embarrassment. He thought it was good and presented at a multi-disciplinary conference in Chicago. He returned from the conference with seventy-five requests for copies of the paper from social workers, doctors, public health people, even pharmacists. That's never happened to me then or ever. He *did* know something that I didn't!

Tony T was easy to write with but not easy to work with. Eventually, we developed our own *modus operandi* for writing books together. He came up with the idea, which we then discussed fully, and I came up with the title. Then he would do a meticulously, if not to say obsessively detailed outline. From that I could write a first draft. If real-world examples were necessary, I would invent them out of whole cloth. My strength was in making complex concepts easy to understand for non-researchers. Then he would clean it up, add the footnotes, and off it would go to the publishers.

In our writing together, I was never first author and never thought I deserved to be. At Michigan, when I was being considered for promotion, he said that for our next book I should be first author and we should reverse roles. It was a disaster. For one thing, I was a single parent and if one of my kids or both got sick, I couldn't keep to our tight writing schedule. He, on the other hand, finished a chapter the night his second wife was having their second baby. I asked him how he could possibly focus and produce a chapter the night his wife went into labor. With that full-faced smile, he simply pointed to his diary and the date we'd agreed upon for his delivery.

A third of the way through, I told him I just couldn't keep to our original contract. No problem; we had a deadline with Columbia Press, so we re-reversed roles. Though I didn't ask for it, he insisted that my name be kept as first author. We met the deadline and published the book. One of the pre-publication reviewers made a point of saying that they couldn't believe that anyone could write a chapter about questionnaire construction in only seven pages and re-read it without success, seeking omissions. Beyond that, I've written only one academic book, solo and that was one he encouraged me to write for an encyclopedic series he conceived of and edited for Oxford University Press.

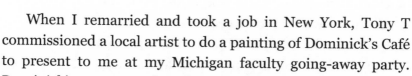

When I remarried and took a job in New York, Tony T commissioned a local artist to do a painting of Dominick's Café to present to me at my Michigan faculty going-away party. Dominick's was an outdoor cafe behind the law school where I liked to hang out when I wasn't teaching or at faculty meetings or in the library. I loved Dominick's tuna heros for lunch and would often have a late afternoon drink or coffee there with graduate students. Good glazed donuts, too. Wine was served in jam jars. Cool for Ann Arbor and the tuna was Italian and packed in olive oil.

The painting was presented to me at the faculty party. I found it, and the presentation by a prominent senior faculty who was probably glad to see me go, very moving and thanked Tony personally and everyone else, though I admit, I liked the café more than the painting. A few minutes later, Tony pulled me aside and again I thanked him and told him how touched I was. He responded that the painting would be worth a lot someday, so if I ever got tired of it he'd be happy to have it back.

Seven years later, when Kayla and I were divorcing, Tony invited me back to Michigan to apply for an endowed professorship. His plan was to become dean when the present dean retired, who was grooming him for the role. I was open to it. More money, less stress, easy Ann Arbor, and a dean who liked me. Even wrote books with me.

Naturally, I needed to give a talk to Michigan faculty about the research and writing I'd been doing since I'd jumped ship in land-locked Ann Arbor previously to return to my native New

York. No problem. Coincidentally, much of the research and writing I was then doing was at Edward's Boysville of Michigan, where I was developing computerized information systems with Tony G, whom I'll tell you about in the next chapter. Tony T and I agreed on a date for my talk and interviews with faculty, some of whom I knew and others who were new to me.

The plan was I'd arrive on a Thursday, and we'd have dinner that night at the Campus Inn. The next morning, I would give my talk. Friday afternoon and Saturday morning, I'd have more interviews and return to New York on Sunday after breakfast with Tony G. So, Tony T would meet me at the hotel on Thursday evening for a leisurely and at the same time academically strategic dinner. Perfect.

When I arrived at the Campus Inn at four, Tony T was already waiting for me at the front desk. He was always early, but never this early. He looked very upset. I was surprised to see him, but we shook hands as we always did and I suggested that I drop my suitcase in my room, wash up, and meet him at the bar for a drink and an early dinner. He said no, that he needed to come to my room now.

When we got upstairs, Tony fell to his knees and started weeping. I thought someone had died. Instead, he informed me that an hour before, the current dean had informed him that he should hire a lawyer, that an affair he was having with a married junior faculty member had come to light, and he couldn't possibly name Tony T. as his replacement.

That left me applying for a job I couldn't possibly get because of my association with Tony T, a lecture to give that I didn't want to give, interviews to have that I didn't want to have, and an incredibly stressful weekend with Tony T, then Sunday breakfast with a different sort of wild man Tony G, and finally, a flight home.

Since at that time, the woman Tony T was involved with was viewed as a consenting adult rather than a powerless victim of Tony T's greater authority, he was ultimately cleared of an ethics charge. That wouldn't happen today.

A few more divorces and marital debacles followed. Kayla and I attended one of his weddings held at the posh Plaza Hotel in an Eastern Orthodox ceremony in which the bride and groom circle each other and place crowns on each other's heads. The bride was a beautiful Turkish American social worker—really smart—whose father was a very wealthy rug merchant. Everyone was beaming. I remember whispering to Kayla, "If he fucks this one up, they'll find him wrapped in an imitation oriental rug floating in the East River." The food was fantastic, and the champagne flowed. The marriage lasted less than a year, but Tony T stayed afloat. As you will see, so did she in his roiling but closeted unconscious.

Ultimately, he became a dean at another Big Ten university. Yet another testament to the veracity of reference letters by people in high places. Contrary to my evidence-based prediction, he did so well as dean there that the university administration abrogated their five-year rule and extended his term to ten. After he retired, I recommended him for a one-year endowed chair appointment at my university in New York. I thought he was too old to do any harm anymore to me. Still, he somehow became entangled with a mature PhD student, but as far as I know nothing terrible happened. *Consenting adults.* Which when you think about both words separately and together means next to nothing.

Truth be told, I breathed a sigh of relief when he left and moved to Long Beach, New Jersey and rented an apartment in a highrise with a view of the Atlantic. He again leased a red Jaguar, his dean car, read novels, watched football, and pined for yet another really smart woman with whom he co-authored a book but who then ditched him for her present husband. Life isn't always fair.

When Fran and I were staying at our beach house in Ocean Grove, he and I would occasionally have dinner together alone in a local seafood restaurant. Fran found Tony T "nice enough, but boring." He would drive his Jag into town and we'd go to the seafood restaurant where he always ordered a steak. I remember thinking when he made eye contact and smiled at the very pretty server that he looked like an infant in a crib seeking a *peekaboo* connection to his mother.

His arthritis was getting worse, but he refused to take painkillers. Hip replacements were out of the question because they would require hospitalization, surgery, and anesthesia. His eyesight was failing but he couldn't tolerate the closeness of an ophthalmologist's eye-pressure gauge—even if she was pretty and very smart. His glaucoma unchecked, he developed Charles Bonnet syndrome and began having visual hallucinations.

The winters alone in New Jersey were too cold and lonely for him, so he was now living in Jacksonville, Florida, a two-hour drive from another one of his sons by his second marriage. Requiring two canes, Tony T would fly in from Jacksonville to attend the Metropolitan Opera with his other New York son and a grandson. He loved the fact that his ten-year-old grandson liked opera as well as soccer. Occasionally, he would send Fran and me tickets to dress rehearsals he was too far away to attend, but I'd have to tell him immediately upon invitation whether we would months in advance.

On his first night in New York, I would always join him for dinner. He would begin with, "Order anything you want, I'm paying." He invariably ordered steak. We each invariably ordered cab-savs. I have my bad habits as well. But I worried about him traveling in winter with his canes. He was too vain to even think of a walker.

The next-to-last time I met him for dinner, it was snowing, and I called the Columbia Club to find out if he'd arrived. When

I was connected to his room, a staff member answered, said he'd arrived but had fallen on his face entering the building. When I got there, his New York son had already arrived and we decided to his great relief that with a blackened eye and cotton stuffed up one nostril, he didn't need an ER.

A year later we tried again. He'd make these dinner dates months in advance and express anxiety about whether I would remember and show up on time. On the subway near the Columbia Club, I got a call from him asking whether I was coming. I was fifteen minutes early. I reassured him that I was a short walk away.

I suggested that we meet in the restaurant because mobility was so difficult for him. When I joined him, he skipped the handshake and immediately told me he was in big trouble, and it was clear that he was hallucinating about past loves following him on the plane and showing up in his room. His son joined us, and I assured him that after dinner I would see him to his room to check things out and his son could return the next morning with the grandson for the opera. The last time I saw or spoke to Tony, it was to reassure him that there was no ex-wife hiding in his room. I did not find this laughable or somehow just. I just found it incredibly sad.

He died in a hospital for patients with dementia near his Florida son. Apparently, and to my surprise, he was quite happy there, took memory classes, and ran imaginary faculty meetings from his bed. The nursing staff loved him and probably nurtured him unconditionally in the way he'd been seeking all his life.

Tony endowed several university lectureships and a student lounge. He published numerous texts, edited an extraordinary series of social work research handbooks, self-published some awful poetry and sentimental travel writing about Italy that sold online to Italian Americans longing for the old country, and wrote some clever essays about his relationship to his canes and short, pleasant essays about his appreciation of art and music. He always thought he could write a great novel if he simply decided to do it. But he never received the career achievement award from his peers he most coveted, even though he was the first president of the organization that awarded it. I believe his conduct of his personal life explained it.

It wasn't until he was showing signs of dementia that I questioned my own culpability in *enabling* his destructive behavior, merely by my listening. For me, his life and death had elements of a Greek tragedy, his many academic achievements upstaged by a trail of seemingly ineluctable interpersonal endings of his own doings and undoings. In *Oedipus Rex*, the blind prophet Tiresias tells our hero, "Creon is not your downfall, no, you are your own." I was not yet nearly blind as I am today, but I could speak and never said that. Should I have?

Yet he died probably thinking that I was his best friend. Maybe I was. Maybe I wasn't. We never hugged. He would have freaked if I tried to. However, if I were a defensive linebacker on an opposing team and brought him down after an end-run with him carrying the ball, he would have smiled, tapped me on my helmet, and said, "Nice play."

On a very different plane, our last time together reminded me of Shakespeare's *Richard III*, when the ghosts of Richard's male conquests return to haunt him on the battlefield. Likewise, Tony T's ghosts of female conquests followed him in the air from Jacksonville to New York.

This story saddens me deeply, but somehow, I don't feel guilty. And I don't miss him the way I miss my brother, who was far less intelligent and far less cognitively complex.

CHAPTER 10

TONY G, "DOC, DON'T YA GET IT?"

TONY G SHOWED up in my master's level Program Evaluation course at the University of Michigan in 1978 just prior to my leaving. It was fated, if not *bashert*. Like so many others before him who sat opposite me in the classroom, we started as competitors and became friends, but I can't say I ever loved him. In his final master's degree year at Michigan, he had already developed a following from the margins of the student body—Chicanos from Texas, rural Michiganders, a couple of ex-cons—not your conventional Ann Arbor, left-liberal tree huggers.

He had the characteristic short and stocky build and darting eyes of a baseball catcher, as though an opposing player might be about to try to steal a base from him. Always on the alert for a wisecrack he could make or a skirt he could "ooh and ah" about. In many ways the opposite of Tony T and in many ways alike.

Also of Italian extraction, Tony G had grown up in Des Moines, had a distinct mid-western twang, and did absolutely nothing to disguise it. With his perpetual broad smile, his persona was not a strong, silent, seductive Boy Scout, but a wise guy. Not the Mafia type from Scorsese films, but the kind of classroom cut-up who was always ready to find a way to make "Teach" look dumb. And yet growing up in Des Moines rather than Detroit, there was also a cornfield innocence about him.

Clearly very smart and organizationally astute, he loved finding logical flaws in the lecture examples I provided, but we never had a personal conversation until I made a passing reference to how I make red sauce for pasta. Only the Pope

knows what that has to do with program evaluation, but it
began a twenty year and enormously productive collaboration
followed by about five years of little or no communication until
just before he died. The after-class test question that he had
for me was when I made pasta with sauce that contained pork
chops and meatballs (or even codfish in red sauce, which he also
classified as "meat in gravy"), did I serve the meat in the same
bowl as the pasta or on the side in a separate bowl? My saying,
"Separate," bonded us for many future years.

Tony G was a computerized information system visionary.
Students in the class were required to do presentations about
evaluation research they could imagine implementing in their
agency field placement, the organization in which they worked,
or even in the school of social work which they currently attended.
I was open to all those possibilities but had no idea what to
expect from Tony G. He scheduled his classroom presentation
strategically for the last day of class. What he presented was a
far-ahead-of-its-time scheme for a computerized information
system that would in real time assess individual and program
outcomes at Boysville, where he worked. This was 1978, far
beyond anything that anyone was even thinking about in social
work services. I was gobsmacked.

When he finished, he just smiled with enormous self-
satisfaction as the class burst into applause. Naturally, I praised
his presentation and to myself thought many less positive
thoughts. "Little bastard" was one. No class ever applauded for
me like that on my final day of class. I wished the class well, to a
smattering of intermittent and muffled claps and sincere smiles.

For Tony G, it was one of the high points in his life thus far
and he beamed and laughed like a happy jackal every time we
revisited that event. He enjoyed it most when I reminded him of
it, but he wasn't shy about reminding me.

Two years later and me back in New York, I received

a telephone call from him asking whether I remembered him. When I heard, "Doc, this is Tony from your program evaluation class," I immediately knew who it was. The sobriquet alchemically combined genuine affection and playful derision. I couldn't help liking this guy. He made it clear, however, that he wasn't calling just to say hello; he wanted to visit and talk about his plans for us to work together.

A few days later, he was sitting in my office saying that he'd like me to come to Boysville to work with him to implement the computerized evaluation scheme he'd presented in class. Gobsmacked once more, Tony G had convinced the administration at Boysville to hire him as research director and fund his innovative scheme. It didn't stop with the necessary computers and the two of us. Tony G's offer included my chairing a National Research Advisory Committee (NRAC) of prominent social work researchers from universities throughout the country who would come to Boysville quarterly. The gaggle would oversee our work and conduct research with the data Tony G's information systems generated. Not with external grants, but with agency funds.

I could not believe his hubris, but I couldn't say no. He made it very clear that he needed my credentials and contacts to legitimate his plan, which would put Boysville on the map as one of the most innovative, research-based social work settings in the country—if not the world. In truth, however, it was also about him crowning himself king of social work computerization. But that was fine with me because I thought what he was proposing was truly visionary and I had no aspirations for the throne. Nor did I have the necessary technical knowhow.

Later I learned that the moneyman behind the throne was Edward of Bob's Beef Buffet fame. Edward was then associate director of Boysville and saw something in Tony G that he believed in. And as irksome as Tony G could get, Edward saw to it that Tony's scheme was funded every year with agency funds leveraged from operating expenses and service grants from the diocese, the state, and the federal government.

Somewhere along the line, though, Tony G decided that to wear the crown, the king needed to get his doctorate. With my genuinely inspired endorsement, he enrolled in the doctoral program in which I taught at Hunter and convinced Edward to fly him in from Detroit once a week for two days of classes, where predictably he made quite an impression on his fellow students with his smarts, his wisecracking, and his braggadocio. Less so on his instructors.

Tony G's favorite expression was, "Don't ya get it?" He'd use it when he thought his thinking was far ahead of the person with whom he was sharing his ideas. He sprinkled it liberally in exchanges with others like salt on French fries, but some of Tony G's professors experienced it like salt on wounds. Calling me Doc was adding ketchup to his fries. I never got through one conversation with Tony G without one, "Doc, don't ya get it?"

When he started the doctoral program, we both agreed for multiple reasons—legitimate and otherwise—that he could waive taking my required research course and substitute something more advanced to keep pace with his manic energy and supercharged intelligence. Let someone other than me put up with a semester full of DYGIs.

Since Kayla and I then owned a large loft with ample room for guests, I invited him to stay with us on the nights he needed. That arrangement had worked well for an entire year when a Japanese doctoral student, Tatsuru, spent one night a week with us rather than commute to the North Fork of Long Island where he, his wife and children rented a house. After telephoning to be sure, Tatsuru would kindly arrive only after Kayla and I finished dinner, bow, and accept a cup of tea, always apologizing for his imposition, convinced that the tea was an accommodation to him and that every other night of the week we had coffee after dinner—which we never did. I gave up trying to convince Tatsuru when I realized that from a cultural standpoint he was required to apologize.

Tony G's tenure only lasted one Sunday night and Monday morning. By lunch I had asked him to find a hotel in future weeks. He drove Kayla and me crazy with his constant talking, requesting Phillips screwdrivers to tighten loosened screws he found, adjustments he needed to make for our TV to suit him, suggestions he made for improving my cooking, and requests for finding the nearest 7-Eleven where he could buy another six-pack of beer.

He took it well, understood completely, and got Edward to finance his subsequent stays in a modest Upper East Side hotel with a bar where he bent the ear of the bartender with talk about women and sports every Sunday and Monday night for the rest of the academic year.

Tony completed his remaining coursework in the excellent organizational psychology department at the University of Michigan, where he could pay in-state tuition and live at home with his wife and daughters, ostensibly a good arrangement for all of them. Prodigiously heterosexual, I remember him once sharing with me that he could "fuck a snake" if someone held it still for him. He failed to add, of course, that the snake had to be female and one with big boobs—that was understood.

He did quite well there in organizational psychology at Michigan and wrote his doctoral dissertation at Hunter about the Boysville program he created without one DYGI at his defense to anyone serving on his dissertation committee—probably my sobering influence. Unlike Eli, Tony G breezed through on a combination of total self-confidence and truly groundbreaking innovation. Though I officially chaired his committee, he needed no help from me on either score.

Once he had his doctorate, he talked Edward and Edward's

superior, Brother Francis, into sponsoring a national invitational conference of prominent social work researchers from throughout the country to be held in Michigan. The conference produced a published collection of papers but nearly cost us our lives driving to it. On treacherous I-94, Tony informed me that he'd invited none of his Boysville research staff to attend the conference. By then he had at least four working in his research unit—one on his PhD—none of whom he said deserved to be at the conference because none had their doctorates. That was the one and only time we ever nearly came to blows.

He was driving very fast on a pitted highway full of semis and because I had a strong urge to live, I made him pull off the road. We started wrestling and slapping each other—with him all the while pleading, "Doc, I need this. DYGI? Let me have this one thing, that's all I ask." I gave in.

The conference went smoothly except for the moment when one invited guest from Wayne State claimed that he was the originator of the Boysville research design. I held Tony G back as the convener of the conference went on to introduce the next speaker.

Our most memorable workshop was held in Canada. Tony convinced a colleague at the University of Calvary to convince the dean to have the school sponsor a four-day workshop for agency administrators on program self-evaluation. It was quite innovative since part of the workshop would be lecture, and the other part hands-on computer using de-identified Boysville data for participants to pursue their own research interests and write reports based upon their findings. It would be held in Chateau Lake Louise, a costly ski resort, and participants would have to pay $450 to attend in addition to their own travel and lodging. It wasn't ski season but that was still a lot of money.

Successful execution of the plan involved bringing Boysville data on magnetic tapes borrowed from IBM with a $10,000 deposit returnable on return. De-identified Boysville data was downloaded on the tapes to upload onto fifteen desktop computers rented for this purpose. There would be a lecture room and a hands-on computer lab where pairs of participants would analyze data, write reports, and in a final session present their findings and policy implications. I would provide the lectures and Tony would do the hands-on in the lab across the hall. The first night, there would be an open bar reception. All paid for in advance by the University of Calgary. Perfect.

Tony G said he would fly in from Detroit on Saturday to play a round of golf with the dean, and I would arrive from New York on Sunday afternoon, when Tony would upload all the data on the waiting computers. Then we'd have a drink, an early dinner at the chateau, and a good night's sleep before the workshop began early the next morning. Perfect.

When I met him at the chateau on Sunday afternoon, Tony didn't look happy. For good reason. When asked, "Tony, why so glum?" he told me that the day before he had backed up a golf cart over the dean's new set of clubs, which would set him back $1,000 and probably wouldn't make him a friend for life of the guy whose name and picture were on the workshop brochure.

The real problem was yet to be discovered. When we went to the lab to upload the tapes, we discovered that the carefully structured and organized Boysville data had been electronically scrambled. It did not take a digital genius like Tony to *post-hoc* diagnose the problem. Getting on the plane he made sure that he carried on his precious carton of cigarettes, his business suit, and his golf attire. After all, he was crossing an international border and making a stop in Toronto to change planes. These important personal accessories could get lost.

What he didn't anticipate was that by belly-loading the computer tapes in a cardboard box with only *Please Don't X-ray—Personal Data* written across with black marker, he all but ensured that the contents would be x-rayed by the security geniuses at either airport. That scrambled all the data, but his cigarettes survived intact. Cigarettes cost a fortune in Canada. If they'd allowed me to carry my Smith & Wesson .45 across the border, I would have shot him right then and there.

We skipped dinner. To his credit, Tony worked until 3 a.m. unscrambling the data and uploading it while at midnight, at his instruction and without push back, I ordered pizzas with extra pepperoni and two six-packs of cold Diet Pepsi to be delivered to the lab. I don't remember which pizza place was open at midnight on a Sunday in Alberta, but I'm grateful they were. By 8 a.m. we'd both slept a couple of hours, but we blamed our shakiness at breakfast on jet lag rather than on all the Pepsi we'd consumed. After we did general introductions and an icebreaker of sorts to gather ourselves, Tony spontaneously decided to read a theoretical paper he had written especially for the occasion on his theory of the binary nature of the universe or something along those lines. Again, I gave.

But Dr. G's lecture was a slowly exploding bomb. Attendees were either bored silly or had no idea what he was talking about. I'm not sure he did. The dean and the faculty member who'd brought us there were panicking and more astute attendees were shaking their heads and thinking about what they'd spent on this debacle. When I couldn't tolerate it anymore, I jumped in and suggested an early lunch break, that perhaps the content was a bit too theoretical for the first day and the most valuable experience of the workshop would be the hands-on portion in the lab across the hall. By then, if it were possible to circumnavigate his thick neck with my bare hands and, had I possessed his computer skills to carry on with the workshop, I would have strangled him. To his credit, at that point he would have offered no resistance.

The first afternoon portion of the workshop involved

introducing participants to the Boysville Management Information System, gracefully named BOMIS, and the input and output data categories contained within. That went quite well; Tony was in his element and pairs of participants were trolling through the data for variables they were interested in on their dedicated computers. They were playing, Tony was cruising, and for the first time in two days I was breathing normally.

About a half hour before the first workshop day concluded and a couple of hours before the planned getting-to-know-one-another reception, a participant raised his hand and asked how, under the BOMIS system we would code a "youngster who was in custody for attempting sex with his neighbor's chickens?"

Tony and I caught each other's eyes and wondered whether this was really happening. He decided to lateral the question to "Professor Epstein, who is a renowned expert on social deviance." After all he had already put me through, no way was I going to touch that question.

"As a New Yorker," I said, "I've had no experience with anything of the sort and I'm not as familiar with BOMIS as Tony, its originator," so I passed it back to him. After giving it his deepest cogitation and attention, he launched into a lecture on labeling theory, victimless crime, and the deeply philosophical and strangely resonant question, "Who was the victim, the chicken or the boy?"

The participants' eyes glazed over, and I announced the location of the reception and the open bar. A giant Canadian sigh filled the lab. I returned to my room to rest and look forward to food and alcohol—mostly the latter. On the way back to our adjoining rooms, utterly exhausted, I felt no impulse to talk to him ever again, but he needed to share with me that one of the female workshop participants wanted to fuck him.

In exasperation, I said, "Nonsense."

"I can see it in her eyes," he assured me.

Classic projection. "Bullshit," I responded.

"You'll see," he said.

At the party, everyone was so relieved from the tension of the day that we all let down. Canadians are drinkers and we all imbibed plenty. I kept my distance from Tony, feeling comfort in the fact that the next morning's session was mine and he seemed to accept that his impromptu reading of his theoretical lecture that morning was lame. But like Tony T before him, Tony G was incapable of apology.

Somewhat juiced by then, I approached a gaggle of participants that included the guy who'd asked about the boy and his neighbor's chickens. I apologized for interrupting—something I had no trouble doing whether drunk, partially drunk, or sober— but asked whether the example he had offered was real. Before he could answer, a woman in the group enthusiastically volunteered, "Oh that's nothing. We had a youngster in our place who was having an *ongoing relationship* with a pig."

Oh Canada, I thought and moved on to another gaggle.

Next morning was breakfast on our own, which I had safely in my room. Returning at 8:50 a.m. to the lecture room to prepare my notes, my jokes, and my PowerPoint presentation, something caught my eye. Can the absence of something or someone catch one's eye? Tony G wasn't present, nor was the woman whom he claimed wanted to have sex with him, so even if I was crazy enough to, I couldn't turn the floor over to him, or to her for that matter. But forgive me, Germaine and Gloria, I worried most about him returning for the afternoon session, which I couldn't possibly conduct.

At 1:50 p.m. Tony showed up wearing his more familiar Jack-o'-lantern smile and a thumb's up for, "I told you so." When I admonished him for skipping the morning session, he said, "Doc, I knew you'd do a great job and here I am, right on time—in fact I'm ten minutes early!" His new bosom pal skipped both sessions, but I wasn't offended and was quite content to have dinner alone in my room for that and the succeeding nights. She showed up the third morning with a shy smile and an apology for missing the previous day, which I was happy to wave away without explanation. The workshop ended remarkably well in view of how it started and received positive, if not glowing, evaluations. To Tony's surprise, but not mine, we were never asked back.

Tony felt he outgrew Boysville and took a teaching job at the University of Nevada, Las Vegas. No surprise, he loved gambling and claimed to have figured out ways to beat the system. On a trip there one weekend, he won $30,000, was chauffeured to the airport, and invited back—flight and hotel on the house. By that time, he had divorced and married a woman with whom he'd had an extramarital affair at Boysville. They married poolside in Vegas. Surely it was none of Boysville's Sisters of Mercy, though I wouldn't have put it past him to try. Mercy has its limits. By that time, I'd reached mine with him but continued my consultation at Boysville.

For reasons I didn't understand, after he moved to UNLV he stopped communicating with me both professionally and personally. When asked why, he said he was writing a book, implying that I probably wouldn't understand it. He needed to do it on his own and wanted to focus on promotion and tenure. He never published his book, never got tenure, and again divorced. He left Las Vegas and returned to his hometown Des Moines to be closer to his mother.

Next, I heard through Boysville sources that he had remarried, but shortly afterwards had been diagnosed with lung cancer. I contacted him to say how happy I was that he found somebody and how sorry I was about the cancer, and asked whether I might come to Des Moines sometime to visit with him. He said he thought that would be great, he'd love me to meet his new wife and see the house they had built together. I could stay with them.

Another former Boysville friend who was an assistant dean in Kansas, a manageable drive from Des Moines, joined us for dinner that first night. I stayed over and Tony G, his wife, and I cooked Italian together the following night. Tony was very proud that his new wife was a corporate executive in fiber electronics and that he was doing organizational consulting. He seemed especially proud that there was a flatscreen TV on the wall of almost every room.

On my last day there, I asked again what had happened between us. His response was predictably, "DDYGI? You were my mentor and at some point, I needed to defeat you." I told him I didn't get it, but he thought somehow it was a universal law. If not universal at least Italian.

Not many months after I visited, I heard he'd died. The cancer had spread to his brain. He lost a good deal of money gambling online, bought three BMWs in one day, crashed one driving home, and left his new wife with lots of debts and no insurance. Apparently, at the funeral his mother made quite a scene about her poor Tony and his *putana* third wife.

I still don't get it, Tony. I still don't.

CHAPTER 11

NICK T, "YOU KNOW WHAT REALLY PISSES ME OFF?"

NICK T WAS a Greek American with a familiar Greek American story. Yes, his father owned a diner and through diligently applied intelligence as well as physical strength, Nick went on to Columbia College on a wrestling scholarship. He was twenty when he graduated. Short, broad, and muscular like Tony G, he also played catcher on his college baseball team. Unlike Tony G, however, Nick T was a keen and extremely subtle social observer—fluent in English, German, and Greek and a reader of the classics.

After college Nick enlisted in the Army, where he was strategically assigned as an intelligence photo interpreter in Berlin for two years. While Nick never mentioned anything about his Army service, I knew he read Max Weber in the original German without Talcott Parson's translation and lengthy explanatory notes. "Unnecessary bullshit," Nick might say.

Returning to Columbia, Nick and I met in 1961, where he went on to receive his PhD in sociology in 1968. The year before, he'd married Bess, a very refined, American-born Greek woman who had been sent by her parents to a classy finishing school and *safe* college for wealthy young women in Manhattan, so she could remain at home with her parents until she married a nice Greek professional. Bess also learned to cook Greek cuisine— exquisitely. She was groomed to be the perfect, assimilated-but-not-too-much, Greek American wife. I'm not sure Nick was what they'd had in mind for her, but he was getting his PhD after all and would eventually become a professor. The christening of his first son was my first Eastern Orthodox experience in an ornate Greek church in Astoria, that neighborhood being the center of Greek life and culture in New York City—then and today.

When I began working on my PhD, Nick had already studied with some of the greats in college—C. Wright Mills, Daniel Bell, Amitai Etzioni, Robert K. Merton, etc. Two years of coursework ahead of me, he worked as a research assistant to Sy, the professor who later co-chaired my dissertation committee and slid down the banister at Fayerweather Hall. Brilliant and flamboyant, Sy was a notorious rake. Consequently, Nick knew lots of insider secrets about his and other male faculty's peccadillos, which he guarded as though they were military secrets.

About nearly everything else, though, Nick was verbally uninhibited. His favorite way to start a sentence was, "You know what really pisses me off?" You needn't respond, "No, Nick, what really pisses you off?" for him to keep on talking. Often, he would write letters to the *Columbia Spectator* about "fraternity hooligans partying and making noise all night while scholars [presumably Nick] were attempting to study in the library." And though compared to me, he was educationally privileged, we each resented *unearned* privilege. Him much more than me.

Nick and I shared a highly refined sense of the absurd, which to my mind is a *sine qua non* for any serious sociologist. So, we spent much of our time together laughing at pomposity and excessive (from our point of view) self-regard. Despite his overt cynicism about institutions and people who embodied those qualities, like organized religion, Nick wrote his PhD on the Norwegian pastors who opposed emigration to the United States on moral grounds, including slavery. Nick was nothing if not cognitively complex.

Living with all his internal contradictions, Nick had a problem with both alcohol and anger. Separate they were a barrier to our closeness, but together they were combustible and exposed a deep and pulsing vein of racism. That almost took our friendship to the breaking point. But we each held on.

We came closest to the brink when we were both students. Nick had wanted to be informed about any parties in Manhattan my then roommate, Arnie (also a sociology graduate student at Columbia), knew of—and certainly those we might be hosting. Though Nick was married and a father by then, he never brought his wife. Instead, his date was a bottle of cheap scotch—Clan MacGregor—and to this day I think of Nick less than fondly every time I see the black, green, and gold label on the liquor store shelf.

One time, Arnie and I gave a party at our $150-a-month, one-bedroom walkup on Columbus and West 95th Street. Naturally, we invited Nick. He came bounding up our four flights of stairs around 11 p.m. with a bottle that never left his hands. There was a table in the kitchen for beer and wine that Arnie and I had purchased, and others had added to it as they entered, but Nick stuck close by his liquid date. Once he and his wee Scottish lass really got into each other, Nick became quite aggressive and insulting, especially toward Arnie's and my friends of color who were there. Ron was an elegant and handsome cellist who'd come to the party from a practice session and parked his cello in its case close by his seat. Nick thought this an affectation and let Ron know that he thought his cello was bullshit. Wisely, Ron ignored him and after several tries at provoking him, Nick lost interest.

I was dating Joanie, a Black woman at the time, so Nick then turned his attention to her. My guess is he thought it an insult couched as a compliment on my behalf. Possibly the other way around. I don't know what he said to her. She never told me. But she left the room crying.

At that point, I asked Nick to leave, but he refused. With a great deal of effort, Arnie and I bodily dragged him out of our apartment where he passed out on the third-floor landing so guests leaving the party had to step around him on their way down. To Arnie's and my great relief, Nick was gone by the time all the guests had left and I took my date home. Nick and I never talked about it. I just avoided him for a while. He never apologized.

That awful incident was one of many ugly, racially inspired, public and private altercations with Blacks as well as Whites that Joanie and I experienced while we were dating. At another party, another close friend, thinking he was being arch and clever, thanked her for "integrating the party." A White woman on the subway crossed the aisle, told her that she looked very nice and honest, and then asked whether she was available for housecleaning. Black men intentionally and forcefully pushed me and stepped on my feet on the subway as well. Joanie was very beautiful and smart and sweet, but I just couldn't cope with all the hostility our being seen together generated. Though it was the '60s, she and I split up on my account. She was the first woman I loved as an adult, but I failed that test miserably.

Nick and I rekindled our friendship and remained friends for a few years more, meeting for thoroughly enjoyable alcohol-free lunches together near the Columbia campus during which he told me what really pissed him off, but we never talked about that party. One memorable day, while walking downtown, we were deciding between Robin Dell's on the west side of Broadway and Tom's on the east—both standard Greek diners. Robin Dell's closed years ago but Tom's went on to fame in the Seinfeld series and, though as mediocre then as it is today, it soldiers on.

I don't remember who preferred which but as we approached Robin Dell's, some guy came crashing through the door, ran to the curb, and copiously hurled his colorful lunch. Nick and I looked at each other and immediately came to a consensus: Tom's.

But no more party invitations for Nick. Those became closely guarded secrets between Arnie and me while we still lived together. Once Nick and I were both married, he began inviting Lyn, my first wife, and me to dinner at his and Bess's place in Astoria. Sadly however, each time, the same alcohol-fueled scenario unfolded.

Dinners started late, on Greek time. By now they had two beautiful, little, Greek American boys. Nick and Bess would greet us warmly. The boys were put to bed. I would bring wine, but Nick would stick to scotch. Drinks would be poured, and Bess would bring out a tray of exquisitely crafted, plated, and delicious *meze*. More drinks followed along with enjoyable and cordial conversation among the four of us. Then soup. More drinks. Nick and Bess might smoke cigarettes in between. When she was pregnant, she stopped both. Nick neither.

When Bess would remove to the kitchen to get the savory main course and feta salad, Nick would pop up and start giving me an unsolicited bone-crushing neck and shoulder massage. When I'd convince him to stop before he did any serious damage to my spine, he'd turn his attention to the chin-up bar separating the dining room and their bedroom and begin doing pull-ups until the food was brought in. If it took Bess a while, Nick's pull-ups continued. At the moment dinner was served, Nick dropped from his perch, scrambled to his seat, and began eating what Bess meticulously served, taking salad out of the communal salad bowl with his hands and exchanging choice cuts of meat from his plate to mine while praising what a great cook Bess was. And she was. But Nick would act like a total boor until he eventually passed out. Bess would already be crying and apologizing. Consoling her, she and I would drag Nick into the bedroom and struggle to get his sodden weight onto the bed.

It made no sense for us to stay for dessert, so Bess would

press homemade baklava on us to take home. On the elevated line to Manhattan from Astoria, Lyn and I would agree, "That marriage can't last."

The next morning, always a Sunday, possibly after church, I'd get a call from Nick at exactly 10:30. "Great time last night, when can we do it again?"

Soon, though, we both left New York for jobs elsewhere. Lyn and I had our son, Dan by then. Nick got a plum job teaching sociology at Cornell, and I moved to Michigan to teach sociology to social work students. He and I lost touch.

Years later, Kayla, my second wife, and I and my daughter, Becs, spent an idyllic (for me) summer on the Greek island of Rhodes. Our accommodations were unexpectedly primitive. No electricity or plumbing—only a well. But grapevines and fig trees were everywhere for the plucking and a beautiful empty beach where you could swim nude in the wine-dark sea was only a half-mile away, once you got past the cow pies in the field between our tumble-down cottage and the beach.

I was in Greek heaven, but Kayla suffered mightily from chronic asthma because the August *Meltemi* winds drove dry and gritty sand particles across the island and into our lungs. We were surprised because Kayla's and my seaside honeymoon in Nerja in the south of Spain the year before had seemed to liberate her breathing and reawaken her sense of smell and taste.

Becs was thirteen at the time and suffered from the total absence of teenage creature comforts. I did my best to compensate by taking Kayla and Becs to the wedding of Princess Diana and Prince Charles on TV in a taverna in the adjoining Lindos, but Becs still promised she would never forgive me for taking her to Greece. And she hasn't. But I fell in love with Greece. Still am. To my ladies, I was a blind and babbling Homer rather than a heroic Odysseus.

While there, though, I couldn't help thinking of Nick. I'd

heard from a social work colleague at Cornell that Nick and Bess and the kids had moved to a teaching job at the University of Manitoba in Winnipeg, Canada. Nick didn't get tenure. So, I took a chance and wrote to him in the sociology department there. I could easily imagine that the winters in Winnipeg really pissed him off. Moreover, I didn't understand his choosing to teach in such an obscure location. Under it all, Nick was a snob and an academic elitist, though he'd never acknowledge it.

Once back in New York, I received a densely typed, blue airletter in return. It began cordially. Against my odds, he and Bess were still together and living with their two sons in Canada. Nick said he'd stopped drinking and smoking when it was discovered that Bess had thyroid cancer, but she was okay now. He had failed to get tenure and lost his teaching job at Cornell because he hadn't published sufficiently and widely—just one edited book on the family in literature. His research passions were always stubbornly esoteric and weirdly principled—nothing quantitative, nothing theoretically mainstream, and nothing concerning social problems. I assumed his drinking was the real reason for his not being promoted and tenured. The image of him at boozy faculty parties suggested a raging bull in a precious china shop.

What startled me in the letter was his saying that his feelings were still hurt because of the time I asked him to leave Arnie's and my party with no explanation. That had to be twenty years before.

Fearful of opening old wounds, I wrote back and discretely offered a diluted explanation and description of what I remembered had happened. I told him that I missed him as well and regretted that so much time had elapsed since we had connected. I was happy for him, for Bess, and for his sons that he had given up drinking and that they both had given up smoking.

Our correspondence trailed off and for multiple reasons—geographical, professional, and otherwise—there was little opportunity to meet again. I didn't go to sociology conferences, and he probably didn't as well. When I went to Alberta with Tony G, I had enough on my hands to not consider a stop in Winnipeg.

———◇———

In 2016, years later and now married to Fran, I had a dream about Nick. Even post-retirement, my anxiety dreams are often about going to the wrong conference hotel, arriving at conference sessions where I am a speaker late or without my presentation flash drive. A variant is arriving at classes for which I have forgotten to prepare on subjects I know nothing about. Standard and boring professional performance anxiety. None of these things have ever happened. Retired now, they can't possibly, but I still have them.

In my dream about Nick, I was checked into a motel for a conference somewhere in Canada and was told by someone that there was a manila envelope left at the front desk for me. I somehow knew it was from Nick and that it contained a manuscript that he wanted me to read, but the desk clerk said she was instructed not to give it to me without him being there. I returned to my room, excited about the prospect of seeing him again, but got increasingly frustrated when he did not show.

After a while and still dreaming, I returned to the front desk, finding another clerk there. He was equally adamant about his instruction as she was and withheld it from me. I began a lengthy plea for the envelope, explaining that the person who left it for me was an old friend with whom I attended graduate school years before and how I was sure he wouldn't mind my receiving it. I assured the desk clerk that once my friend arrived, I would return to the desk with him, acknowledge that I had pressed and persuaded the clerk to hand over the envelope, and only I would be blamed for the violation of instructions. I was sure, I said, that my friend would think nothing of it.

Even in the dream, I remember thinking my pleading was fulsome and embarrassing. Still, it made no difference.

I was agitated when I awoke. Though I am ostensibly a person of science, I thought it was a message from Nick. It was. When I Googled him that morning, I learned that he had died the year before, but in 1991 had issued his seminal work, a slim volume entitled *Mea Culpa: A Sociology Of Apology And Reconciliation*, published by Stanford University Press.

Immediately, I went online and posted the following to Bess on *Passages* in the *Winnipeg Free Press*:

> "Dear Bess. Last night (2/6/16) I dreamed that I was in a motel where I'd received a manuscript from Nick who was staying in the motel, but the management refused to connect me with your room. We hadn't been connected in years, since he began writing 'Mea Culpa.' In the dream, I complained to multiple levels of management with no success. In total frustration, I told them I would write to the New York Times about it. To no avail. As you know we hadn't seen each other since graduate student days at Columbia. So, I rushed to the computer with hopes of e-mailing and the first citation that came up was this obituary. It deeply saddened me. I am so, so sorry about yours and your family's loss. I just ordered his book and will read it with sadness while trying to remember the joy he emanated."

I signed my name with love and condolences but never received a response. Eagerly I ordered the book to download to my Kindle. As anticipated, the book is gorgeously written, elegantly formatted, and broadly researched though concise in length. It was grounded in ancient Greek philosophy as well as in everyday contemporary experience.

What I didn't anticipate was that the book's beginning:

> "*I trace my interest in apology* [author's italics] to a bitter dispute I had many years ago with someone close and dear to me. The precise details have faded from memory, but I can still recall feeling hurt, wronged, and angered by the accusations of misconduct and insensitivity. Moreover, the charges seemed to go beyond my alleged transgression. They not only reflected (in my eyes) a harsh judgement of my character but also struck at the very core of our relationship. As our disagreement grew more heated, I finally said that nothing less than a 'full and sincere apology' would clear the air and set things right between us and it really didn't matter in the light of my agitated emotional state. The day after this painful encounter I received a short letter expressing sorrow and asking for my forgiveness. At our next meeting the apology was repeated orally and after I accepted it, we both agreed to forget the matter."

Although Nick had no recollection of his transgression, he remembered the incident and his feeling deeply aggrieved for all those years. I have no recollection of ever apologizing to him orally and certainly not in writing for *my* behavior or for my asking for forgiveness, but I can easily imagine expressing my desire to patch things up as being well within my motivation and social skill set. On opening the book on my Kindle, I hoped for a mini-second that it was written in *apology to me* for the hurt he caused Joanie, my date, and me. Sociologist though he was, *Nick was still Nick,* I thought. But was he?

Still, old men forgive as well as forget and I am indeed an old man.

Going on, Nick says:

> "Sometime later, I recalled this poignant incident when something I said (or done) jeopardized a cherished friendship and moved me to apologize to redeem myself. The reminder of this incident and other similar incidents somehow stirred my curiosity about the nature of apology. Was it possible that this mundane, yet mysteriously potent, symbolic act had something important to tell us about social life?"

Indeed, it did, Nick, indeed it did. And whether you apologized to me or I apologized to you no longer matters. Like every excellent sociologist (or novelist, for that matter), you turned your wound and consequent rage into something valuable for us all—a gift that sadly ties me to your memory.

GEORGE W. DOWNS
(1946-2015)

CHAPTER 12

FOR THE LOVE OF THREE GEORGES, WHAT'S IN A NAME? NOTHING AT ALL

IN MY LIFE, I've loved three Georges. All devotedly. None carnally. Other than their given names, they were nothing alike. Each had a side I knew well and another barely.

George D was my first George and easily the smartest man I ever knew. When we met in the early '70s, I was a rookie professor, recently transplanted to Ann Arbor from New York and he a rookie PhD student from Chicago via Korea and a stint in the Air Force. He'd been hoping to fly fighter jets, but a previously undetected seizure disorder ended that. Instead, while in Asia, he read poetry in Kyoto and practiced meditation.

Never really only student-teacher, we played Sunday softball with pick-up teams of oldish students and youngish professors. Six-foot-three and lanky, with a graceful Ted Williams swing, he lofted fly balls effortlessly into the outfield. I hit line drives. He loped, I trudged. He naturally gravitated to first base but played it contemplatively. I was a scrappy, scatter-armed second baseman by default. Whether dropping pop-ups or muffing ground balls, I routinely threw over his head or under his knees, evading his stretch. From teammates I got catcalls. From him, a comforting hand on my aching shoulder.

Not quite a giant, but always gentle.

Our centerfielder was Ted, another PhD student who would eventually move to California for a distinguished career in social welfare and aging policy. But at the time, while we were all youngish *whatevers* and living in Ann Arbor, the three of us were inseparable—even collectively falling in love with Lisa, the incredibly cute and pretend-worldly lead singer and country fiddler of the Honky Tonk Angels. They played Tuesdays at Bimbo's, a pizza joint famous for their weekend oompah band, kids' birthday parties, and empty peanut shells thrown on the floor.

Each time Lisa sang her version of Kitty Well's signature, "It Wasn't God Who Made Honky Tonk Angels," we fell in love with her all over again and didn't mind showing it one bit. Nor did we give a hoot whether Herschel, the band's leader and Lisa's putative boyfriend, knew it.

Though we all fell in love with Lisa, we never fell out *over* Lisa or current girlfriends or wives or ex-wives. In fact, after Lyn and I separated, I moved in with Ted above a different Ann Arbor pizza joint run by Greeks who returned to their home island every summer to throw dollar bills from their rented convertible to the locals. Their restaurant exists to this day but it's not worth naming. My kids spent weekends with me there with Ted, and a half century later my daughter still lunches with Ted at UCLA where she works and from which he is a retired dean.

One story that I love about the three of us—George D, Ted, and me—happened while George was at UC Davis and Ted was living in San Francisco and working at a gerontology research center in Berkeley. I flew from New York to San Francisco, and Ted and I planned on driving to Davis to spend the day and have dinner together at George's favorite French restaurant.

How happy Ted and I were cruising over the Golden Gate Bridge in Ted's mustard yellow Porche convertible, singing along with the Eagle's *"don't let the sound of your own wheels drive you craaaazy"* as loud as we could. Intending to recapture the softball glories of our past, Ted and I had both brought our mitts and a ball, but we had no bat. We figured either George would have one or we could easily buy one in Davis.

We met at George's place, changed to a slightly more

commodious car, but still had no bat. "No problem guys," George said. There were three sporting goods stores in Davis. We drove to each one and were dismayed that all they sold were aluminum bats that made that awful ping sound when you hit the ball. We collectively hated that sound. On our third try—and fearing that we had struck out—we approached the store owner and asked plaintively whether he had a wooden softball bat that we could buy.

He looked at us with a rueful smile and asked, "How long since you guys played softball?"

Momentarily defeated, we went threesies on an aluminum bat and headed to an empty softball field George knew of. On the field, we played a ridiculous version of three-man softball with pitching, hitting, throwing and running bases—even sliding. Three PhDs and total idiots. I have no recollection of how we concocted rules of the game, but I remember all of us limping and dragging our throwing arms when we returned to George's car.

After a wonderful dinner, our return back over the Golden Gate was less boisterous but equally happy.

———————<>———————

In a similar manner to how I got "chosen" to play second base, I was on George's political science and social welfare PhD committee by default. He needed a fifth. The others were heavy hitters in organizational and political theory. I was a convenience. A designated hitter. For me, it was an honor and a thrill. George D was so very smart. And he knew it.

Weeks before his defense, after reading his dissertation, I met with him in my office and suggested a modest change in the final chapter. He flashed anger at me for the first and last time, calling my suggestion nonsense. With no additional input from me and giving no heed to my critical insights, his manuscript was published as his first book—a case study in bureaucracy and innovation.

In the years following our undistinguished softball careers, George D took an entry-level teaching position in political science at Davis and before long, left as a full professor for a named chair at the Woodrow Wilson School at Princeton. Well before that, social welfare disappeared from his CV and his persona. Even before Davis, his sights morphed from a career straddling social work and political science to a career straddling political science and international law. And it was a splendid and distinguished career he fashioned for himself.

From an early focus on American social welfare policy, he smoothly shifted to international politics. Not trashy electoral politics, but disarmament theory, nation building, treaty compliance, and the prerequisites of democratization. Applied mathematics as well—Wikipedia describes him as a "pioneer of the application of non-cooperative game theory to international politics."

He retired a distinguished professor of politics at NYU and a former dean of social sciences. We'd remained friends over the years, but my return to New York to teach at Hunter and his move to NYU was a boon to our relationship. A bachelor for much of his life, before moving to New York, he married Ilene, a woman he'd met at Princeton.

Ilene, George, Fran, and I occasionally had dinners together at their NYU apartment on Washington Square West or at Square North, a restaurant across the street where Fran knew the owner from years back at Mount Sinai and encouraged her to take the gamble. When it was just the two of us—George D. and me—we routinely dined at Po on Cornelia Street.

Mario Batali had famously started there and moved on. But Po was good enough for us. George D was nothing if not generous. Notwithstanding his tipping, he was loved by everyone there from busboys to bartender. We both flirted shamelessly with a pale and diminutive artist-server who wore Victorian lace dresses and had an extremely scary goth website. We each visited her website only once.

George D possessed a delightfully mordant sense of humor. If I said I was depressed, he'd immediately say, "Of course!" Over dinners, we'd happily share a bottle of Lachryma Christi. Of course! He expressed interest in whatever I had to say and taught me to say the word *adore*. He adored many—particularly his former PhD students. I'm sure they adored him.

We talked books, electoral politics, and matters very personal. However, he had to be coaxed into talking about his research. I suspect he thought I wouldn't understand its complexity. But when I chanced upon a surprisingly apposite question, he'd light up and let it rip. Those were, for me, our happiest times together. Unlike Chef Mario, we always left Po laughing.

George D died of neck cancer, years after disfiguring facial surgery, salivary insufficiency, and other bodily humiliations. In my last photo of him, he posed with a Kleenex box on his head. Eileen thought it undignified, but arguably his death was more so. At least the Kleenex box was his choice. I was extremely upset about the circumstances surrounding the final months of his life and choices Eileen made—but George agreed to—like moving to a location where he could no longer walk across the park to his office and chat with former colleagues. He and I could no longer walk to dinner at Po.

In the end, George and I were left alone only once long enough for me to tell him how much I loved him. In that conversation, he mouthed to me, "I hate it here." For years, I couldn't jettison my anger about how and where he died. It led me to a grief therapist where I had to acknowledge that he participated in the decision to move, and where.

Ted's and my relationship has been somewhat strained ever since. I no longer am in contact with Eileen. Fran, who was never close to Ilene, honors my decision. Ted and his wife see Ilene whenever they are in New York or she is in Los Angeles. What do you owe a friend and what do you owe his widow?

Po no longer exists. Mario is no longer a celebrity chef.

And the last time I ate at Po I brought news of George's death and a stamped, addressed sympathy card for staff to sign and send to Eileen—more for them than for her. I ate alone and pictured him opposite me sharing the sweetbreads that we both adored and a bottle of Lachryma Christi. Of course.

In his memory, I planted a flowering plum tree in front of our weekend house in Ocean Grove, where I can talk to him any time I want for as long as I want. It's just outside my window as I write this.

GEORGE ZISKIND
(1928-2014)

Unlike George D, George Z was a curmudgeon. The word was invented for him. Like most curmudgeons, he was a closeted romantic. We met at Hunter School of Social Work in the '80s where he practiced a furious form of word processing in what was then known as the typing pool. Stocky and red-bearded, he never wore a short-sleeved shirt. Later, I learned why. His right arm was grossly swollen with lymphedema, which came from hypodermic needle punctures and collapsed veins.

Already a heroin addict in college in his native-born Chicago, he didn't finish off himself or his schooling. He never spoke of his parents. I never asked. But after flunking out of college he graduated to the federal penitentiary at Lexington, Kentucky, for selling drugs to a narc. He acknowledged that college hadn't taught him much.

But prison did. A gifted, self-taught jazz pianist, he waxed nostalgic about prison as the happiest three years of his life— "a mere kid, locked up with the greatest jazz musicians." Guys whose playing he idolized, he could breakfast, lunch, or dinner with. How cool was that?

Later in life, he mastered his own jazz versions of the *Great American Songbook*, putting all those romantic words, feelings, and wit together with his own jazz stylizations. And he was good. So good, that he became known on a first name basis by many famous jazz pianists. George Shearing was one, but George S is not one of my Three Georges.

For George Z, piano and computer keyboards were extremely different instruments. He played the former like Shearing and the latter like Rachmaninoff. I let him near my new laptop only once and never again. His version of *the quick brown fox jumps over the lazy dog* was more like the "War of 1812 Overture" with cannon fire emanating from the speaker and fireworks on the screen.

But when Fran and I had a party, he was welcome to her piano. After a few drinks and some food, he would sit and play softly and beautifully, but only if we didn't ask. Otherwise, it was a gig for which we should have offered to pay.

George Z met his wife Arlyne in rehab. She'd kicked painkillers through yoga and a total change of lifestyle. She had been a beautiful, young modern dancer, but a wildly unnecessary and terribly botched nose job broke her spirit and ruined her career. Ultimately, she became a yoga instructor and managed her disappointment quite well until she died of breast cancer.

His was a different story. Methadone helped him kick his post-prison heroin habit and he bragged about being in the first cohort of the first successful clinical trial in New York. After years of having to go to a methadone clinic daily, he was trusted with his own monthly supply. Still, he maintained a junkie's mentality until he died about five years after his wife.

By choice and wisdom, they never had children, but they loved cats. For a while they had a store on the Upper East Side called *Purrfection* (he named it) that sold novelty items for other cat lovers. It lasted about three years—same as his prison sentence. Years later, he admitted to me but never to Arlyne that the business did well but "the profits disappeared up my nose." Many more years later, Con Edison caught up with him for unpaid electric bills. He had no idea how they found him; he left no forwarding address and figured if he didn't respond they might think he had died. Anyway, the store had closed, so why were they bothering him?

In telephone *corn alerts*, he spoke of scoring an extra couple of ears of first corn at the farmer's market—"A baker's dozen," he'd say. Once he disguised a pint of Häagen-Dazs as an on-sale substitute at D'Agostino's. "How dare they charge twice as much for something just as good?"

Despite all his bluster and conning, he had a sweet and tender side. While Fran—he called her "Franny Wanny"—was having a bone-marrow transplant for leukemia and confined for a month in a Laminar Air-Flow room, she listened often to a tape he had made for her of him and his favorite pianists to help her pass those brutal, painful, and isolated hours. In fact, she was on the phone talking to "Georgie Porgy" while she was receiving her host sister's life-saving bone marrow via drip from a plastic bag.

Like George D, he loved my kids but only knew them as adults and always asked about them. We would go to Chinatown to the Hoo Lok Corporation where we'd always argue about what to order and then always settle on the classic—cold noodles, orange beef, and dried sautéed string beans with minced pork on top. I'd say, "Improvise."

He'd say, "Why, when you have perfection?"

I'd give.

Now that would be impossible; Mama Hoo Lok and the corporation is gone, George Z is gone, and my kids don't eat meat.

In his '60s, he was still hustling for gigs. Fifty dollars, a meal, and a couple of alcohol *tastes* were his minimum. For a more lucrative event he'd booked, I took him to Mr. Mak, a former Hong Kong tailor I knew on Madison Avenue who refabricated a store-bought blue blazer from Sim's to accommodate his swollen arm. In the right dim lighting, it looked like any other sleeve. It cost more than he earned that night, but he adored that jacket. Mr. Mak's and Sims' no longer exists, but Marcy Sims continues to plug public television. Good for Marcy.

His final gig was one he'd agreed to before learning it required climbing a ladder to a piano loft. Already shaky and in his late '70s by then, he was too proud to back out. Going up was fine, but after a couple of tastes, plus secondary smoke, the descent was a humiliation.

When he was diagnosed with lung cancer soon after, he railed at the injustice because he never smoked tobacco, or so he claimed.

After a couple of surgeries, he began losing weight dramatically and I visited him at his rent-controlled East Side apartment with a living room large enough to accommodate his grand piano and enormous, catalogued CD collection, with hardly any kitchen. *How dare they increase his rent every two years with a kitchen this size?* He and Arlyne did a lot of takeouts. More after she died. He loved his cat as much as I was allergic to it.

One night, however, he telephoned to ask a favor. Could I come across town and buy him a pint of Haggy, preferably strawberry? I bought him two. Answering the door in now-much-too-big, red, plaid pajamas he got on sale from L.L. Bean, he thanked me, asking how much and offering to pay. I told him next time.

One morning shortly after, his cleaning woman found him dead. He'd died in his sleep, I hope dreaming of strawberries. Can someone OD on Haggy's? If anyone could, it would be George Z.

GEORGE GETZEL
(1942-2018)

George G and I began as work colleagues. For years I was a researcher while he was a social group work instructor and HIV/AIDS activist. We admired each other politely from the distance our specializations created.

One day, well after losing both George D and George Z, I was leaving my grief therapist's office and thinking about going to the movies to clear my head when I received a mass email from George G. He had pancreatic cancer and was leaving Hebrew Home and Hospital on the Upper West Side that day for Calvary

Hospice. He requested visitors there.

For me, in that perfect and poignant moment of choice, both Hebrew Home and the film I wanted to see were each a short bus ride away. The movie was across town on East 86th Street and George G was uptown on Amsterdam Avenue. I don't remember the title of the film. It couldn't have been that compelling. For reasons unclear, I chose uptown. That's when I met and came to love George G.

I knew his wife Jessica had died of cancer a year before. He had an adult son—also named Daniel—who was married and had small children and an adult daughter. Both were devoted to him but in that moment unavailable. He had an hour alone before his ride. I helped him pack. But we had such fun laughing about his going to Calvary that I agreed to visit regularly. The irony and appositeness of a Jew leaving Hebrew Home to die at Calvary would make us giddy. But who knew that Calvary was way the hell in the East Bronx—a long and tedious subway and bus ride away? I didn't but discovered it was well worth the ride.

On my first visit to Calvary, I told him about George D and George Z, fearing him suspecting I was seeking a *corrective experience*. George G had known the notoriously cantankerous George Z from the word processing room but had no idea that Z and I were friends. He found that delightfully incongruous. So, did I. George G knew Fran from her student days, adored her, and could easily appreciate why I did as well.

George G thanked me for telling him about the impact of those two losses and shared a lasting grief he held for Diego, a former student and more, who had died of HIV. No stranger to loss as an AIDS activist, clinician, consultant, and volunteer at Gay Men's Health Crisis and other organizations, George G had attended many funerals. There had been rumors about his close relationship with Diego, but that was of no consequence to me. More generally whether he was straight or bisexual mattered little as well. We never discussed either his or my sexual orientations. But in the brief time we knew and came to deeply love each other, we discussed far more important things than where we put our respective penises.

Our weekly visits were replete with old vaudeville jokes, talk about his childhood in the Bronx and mine in Brooklyn, Yankees and Dodgers (Brooklyn only), our children, classical music, opera, expressionist painting, Hitler's Degenerate Art exhibit, and gay gossip he'd garnered from God-knows-where? Did I know that George and Ira Gershwin were lovers? No way! (Yet another George?) Lenny Bernstein, okay! Our favorite places in Chinatown and on Arthur Avenue in the Bronx, where he and his family were close for years with an Italian family who ran a famous bakery.

We talked about Jessica's death and the last time he saw her alive in the Albert Einstein Hospital across the road—same bus stop. He told me about how Jessica returned to him in dreams. His son, Daniel, was married to a lovely Asian woman and their two children were so bright. He lit up as her told me stories of their cleverness. They all visited as often as they could. As did his daughter, who was struggling with her own serious health issues.

We commented about why our daughters never married— mine a PhD in film studies, working in a Chicano Research Center at UCLA, his a benefits advisor for a predominantly male trade union, which she joined as a construction worker until an accident moved her behind a desk. Both beautiful, clever, and witty, and in jobs requiring explanation. We laughingly and simultaneously agreed that they never married because they never met men as smart, interesting, sensitive, and modest as their fathers.

We talked about people we loved and people we hated with remarkable congruence.

We talked opera, Mozart, Shubert, "The Trout," Gilbert and Sullivan. We talked film—Antonioni, Truffaut—Bergman, of course. Lumet's *Bye Bye Bergman*. We talked books. Dostoyevsky and Tolstoy, Murakami, Joyce, Proust, Shakespeare, Beckett, Bert Lahr, and Barbara Pym. What was a Pimm's Cup anyway?

During one of our visits, the Arthur Avenue bakery owner's son, a twenty-something *Ant'ny,* came by to visit. A very different kind of Tony. He called George "Uncle George" and their shared affection was obvious. We all told stories about past family connections to Jewish and Italian gangsters (mine both) but strategically kept the discussion historical and away from the present.

On a subsequent visit, an on-staff rabbi appeared in Calvary, and we told Jewish jokes with Yiddish punchlines, ate chopped liver and herring that I had brought at George's request from Zabar's, and drank Paddy's Irish Whisky that brothers of the Irish guy who'd died in the next room left with George. The rabbi's jokes were awful, but his attempts at profundity landed flatter. When he left, George and I returned to talking about Chinese restaurants on the Upper West Side that had closed. The presence of the rabbi had interrupted that line of profundity.

A week before his last birthday, my wife and I attended a Beethoven Quartet concert. I told him about it. He asked, "What number?"

I said, "Sixteen."

He presciently said, "The final."

Talking birthday instead, I offered cake. He countered with eclairs. We discussed bakeries. I Googled *Eclairs near me.* Arthur Avenue? No way. Too far. Too Italian. The following week I went to L'éclair on the Upper East Side. The saleswoman asked if I needed help. I regret telling her I was there to buy someone's last eclairs. She backed away.

With what I now knew of his flavor preferences, I selected four—one for each movement in Beethoven's 16th. Delighted, he could only manage one bite of each. I followed his lead. We agreed that the pistachio was not as *vivace* as it could have been. Carefully closing the box, he put it aside for the staff.

On my final visit, he was in a sleep from which he wouldn't wake. I asked a nurse if I could see him. She hesitated, then asked if I was the one who brought the eclairs. I nodded and so did she. He was sleeping peacefully. I told him that I loved him and kissed his forehead. What a gift he had given me.

------------------◇◇------------------

My Hong Kong PhD student Wallace Chan did his dissertation on what constitutes a good death for cancer patients in a Hong Kong hospital. As one can imagine, this is no easy subject to study both ethically and methodologically. Wallace employed clinical data mining, the methodology I proposed and wrote a text about published by Oxford University Press in 2009, to study the charts of over eight hundred patients after they had died. In the course of his study, Wallace unearthed what he named the *support paradox,* by which he meant that a good death was not only pain free, psychologically and spiritually unburdened, and with supportive loved ones close by, but a key added element was the patient in turn offering support to loved ones *as* they passed. The support could be practical (like parting business advice) or emotional (like offering forgiveness) or a combination of the two (like a favorite and heretofore guarded recipe for soup dumplings).

Wallace thought his findings only applied to Hong Kong Chinese people. I argued that they were universal—one might easily substitute *kreplach, pierogi, tortellini*...for the soup dumplings. Love and loss are universal.

George G's special gift to me was the opportunity to witness and share his *good death* with total and unswerving generosity. I thank him daily for that gift. Somehow it completes me.

How is it possible that there were three men in my life all given the same name, each so different, yet all so important to me? Each of their deaths represented a different kind of loss, a loss of what could have been. The possibility of loving and being loved. I can never ask them what it was about me that they found appealing. But *mutatis mutandis,* meaning *in consideration of the respective differences,* in age, appearance, longevity of friendship, and circumstance, I think I am the same person. Maybe a bit more mellow and much creakier.

In the very brief epilogue, I'll attempt to explain what it was about them and, perhaps more intriguingly, what differentiated them from the other men I was close to but couldn't love.

But first, Jerry.

JERRY F. CATALDO, PHD
OUTDOORSMAN, PSYCHROLOGIST (SIC), EXPLORER
STILL LOVING FRIEND
(BORN, 1940)

CHAPTER 13

JERRY...NOW, "HI JERRY."
"OH HI, IRWIN!"

JERRY AND I spoke on the phone as we do every week. He is eighty-two and I am eighty-five. At this writing, we've known each other intimately for seventy years and counting. He lives in Buffalo, and I live in New York. In 2018, to celebrate our years of our friendship, Fran and I went to Buffalo where Jerry and I hosted a dinner party for his closest friends. Fran had never met Jerry or seen Niagara Falls. Until then, neither of her two husbands had taken her there. I made an honest woman of her. Jerry and I cooked together for the first time. Pasta, of course.

Jerry came to Ocean Grove once about three years earlier. We both still love the beach but observed no shenanigans. Ocean Grove is a historically Methodist community. Alcohol is not sold, and hanky-panky outside the home is strictly prohibited. As of August of 2022, same-sex weddings are still not performed, but gay homeowners and their guests can now march as a proud group in the July 4th parade. And they do. Also, the restaurants are now BYO. That's progress.

Jerry and I haven't seen each other since the Covid-19 pandemic began. We don't do Facetime, with the rare exception of special events with grandchildren. We're both scared of technological advance, and even more of variant mutations— him more so than I—so we make no plans. But no matter what we talk about, each weekly conversation ends with an emphatic, "I love you, Jerry," and, "I love you, Irwin." Only the order varies.

Our conversations now are not so different as our

conversations then. Naturally, an added component is
daughters, sons, and grandchildren. But what is really precious
to both of us is that when we talk about our parents, we each
can picture what they looked and sounded like—even that single
moment when my father talked to Jerry's in our driveway, mine
poking his finger into Sam's chest to drive home his point and
Sam looking down at Joe's finger silently, while Jerry and I
played stickball in the street.

We talk about women we loved and women we currently
have the hots for. We both can still fantasize. Jerry about JoAnn
Falletta, conductor of the Buffalo Symphony Orchestra and
awfully cute. Me about Sascha, the charming craft therapist
with a Viennese accent who makes tie-dyed scarves with Fran
when she gets chemo. But Jerry remains true to a woman he has
known and loved for many years (who now has cancer), and I
leave the room soon after Sascha arrives looking and sounding
like some combination of a much-more-attractive Lotte Lenya in
the *Three-Penny Opera* and *Mother Courage,* with her cart full
of craft projects or a book of Mary Oliver poetry to read to Fran.
I do this so we can each concentrate on what we are supposed
to be doing and I can resist the impulse to try to charm Sascha.

My fantasies are more literary than Jerry's, whose are more
acrobatic. He was, after all, a gymnast, and what are conductors
if not musical gymnasts? But his fantasies are more outdoors—
snowshoeing with JoAnn. It's obvious. He's the outdoorsman.
Mine are indoors. *Sachertorte mit schlag* and Sascha at a café
in Vienna. Mine change more frequently than Jerry's—always
have. But we are both harmless old men now and at least tried
to be harmless then.

Jerry is a retired academic who still has a thriving private
practice as a clinical psychologist—all now over the phone.
He doesn't do telepsychotherapy. I am a retired academic and
international research consultant with the occasional online gig

in Hong Kong or Melbourne. If only I could go there again. Time differences on Zoom make me crazy. I used to be able to sleep them off.

Though Jerry was trained as a mechanical engineer, and I started my career as a quantitative researcher, we are both hopeless with most digital devices and on-screen sets of instructions. Though we think we are eminently logical, their logic eludes us. A telephone offer by a tech person to walk us through an online procedure is to us like Dante offering us a tour of every circle.

Jerry remains a hunter, a skeet shooter, a sailboat owner and sailor, a snowshoe walker, a collector of shotguns, and an apostate former member of the NRA. He will pass these skills and experiences and the humane attitudes he brings to them to his grandchildren. Though arguably equally humane, I have none of Jerry's skills to pass on. My legacy to my grandchildren comes in the form of pasta and meatballs and quirky stories that they can roll their eyes about.

Jerry and I each blame Trump and Trumpism, Covid and Covid profiteers for all the world's ills—with the exception of cancer, which took away so many of those we loved and threatens even more. Just yesterday we talked about how though heart attack is still the number one cause of death, cancer feels so much more evil and vindictive.

We apologize to each other easily for even the most minor infractions—a call too early or a couple of minutes late. There are no major or even minor infractions.

But before telling each that we love each other, we inevitably finish our conversations laughing with mutual appreciation and gratitude that though we are so different, we understand each other each so completely and so intimately.

Recently, in the spirit of fact-checking this book, I asked Jerry whether in the seventy years we'd known and loved each other, we'd ever had sex together. In my recollection, the closest we'd ever come was witnessing that torrid episode blankets away from us on our separate towels at Jones's Beach—more than a half-century ago.

Knowing that his answer would be "no," but without missing a beat, he surprised me by pausing and adding speciously, "I don't think so. I think I would have remembered it if we had." Then pausing for a pregnant moment, he said, "No, but there's still time."

I thought, *That's the funniest thing Jerry's ever said to me. I need to save that for the end of my book.* Still laughing together, we each said, "I love you. Talk to you next week."

REM DIFFERENTIAM?

THIS COMING-OF-OLD-AGE BOOK originated as something of a memoir and ended, I realize, as a *menoir*. Its purpose was to memorialize the men I've deeply loved over the course of my life and consider the question of why I loved some and not others with whom I worked closely and in many respects was quite intimate. But before I could allow myself to wholeheartedly tell the stories of those I loved, I needed to get past my father's extreme homophobic fear—a fear that he projected onto me from a very early age. That toxic legacy is an essential part of *my* story.

A close reader of the chapter about my father thought he didn't sound all that scary. Trust me, though he only hit me once—and I can't say about my siblings—the dread he inspired in all of us was real. The damage done was real.

Sometimes the threat of abuse is worse than the act. With my sister, the abuse took place without the threat—that was even worse. And did more damage. But that is her story to tell.

Not insignificantly, well after my father died, an unusually honest conversation with my brother revealed that we each grew up thinking the other was his favorite son. No small achievement. But one to which I'm sure many can relate.

I know in some ways publishing this story would be far more propitious if I were gay. At least, I did not have to struggle to meet my *authentic identity* against external and institutional prejudice. And I am White.

But my father's homophobia still cost me inordinately as I ventured out of our small brick house in Flushing, Queens, and into the world beyond it, seeking a meaningful academic career as well as the intimacy with friends and colleagues and partners and children that makes life worth living.

Writing this book has been liberating of the burden of my father's fear as well as other more felicitous encumbrances. Having spent my career writing books and articles about social work research, it is an unanticipated pleasure not to be required to end every chapter with a section on implications for social work practice, policy, or future research.

Once I began this book, another friend who knows me well said I seemed *unleashed*. That was an unfortunate choice of words because my clueless father had once unleashed Ginger, a dog of ours, on the roof and said, "The dumb dog just jumped over." Nothing was ever his fault.

So instead, I told my friend, I prefer *unfettered*.

From the start, however, I worried about fairly and humanely telling the stories of those I could not love. I leave the judgement about how well I've achieved that to readers—especially those who knew and loved them. If I have been unfair, I apologize. I am no arbiter of who to love and who not to. I am, however, an unapologetic advocate of love.

Sociology is about typology. I began thinking about this book as something of a *comparative case study,* though by no means am I offering it as scientific or objective. It couldn't be more subjective. In fact, I would say that my *method* was my subjectivity. The problem that I was left with, however, was how do I explain to myself and to the reader the *rem differentiam* between these two crude groupings of complex men and the deep feelings of love or defense they engendered.

Was what made the difference their grievous childhood wounds; their rigid narcissism; their distorted notions of generosity; their incapacity for empathy; their unacknowledged and various needs for power, alcohol, the trappings of the academy; their childish romanticism, sexual addiction...? I could go on. No combination of any of these describes the difference between those I loved and those I could not.

And yet, for me, pictures tell it all—two at the beginning and one at the end of this book.

The first is a passport picture of D.H. Lawrence. You may think it unfair of me to employ as illustrative of anything a passport picture of an unquestionable giant, an innovator of the modern novel. Still, almost everyone who knew him agreed that Lawrence was a crashing, narcissistic bore—the combination of he and his wife, Frieda, even worse to be around.

In shape and form however, it reminded me of the picture I took of George D on the last day I saw him alive. We both knew the end was near. It hovered over us, but we were not alone enough and George D generally eschewed hugging.

When Fran suggested a picture, George D at first declined. Then he lit up as he inevitably did and, removing to his study, took a pose with a Kleenex box on his head. The pose was entirely his idea.

The picture at the end of the book is of Jerry wearing a pith helmet on the day I gave him the definitive biography of Sir Richard F. Burton, the famous British explorer, linguist, and translator of the Kama Sutra. Jerry loves books about explorers. Not so much about linguists. And who doesn't like the Kama Sutra?

That pose was my idea. For reasons beyond my comprehension he had a pith helmet on the backseat of his car—doesn't everybody?—when he picked me up at the airport in Buffalo. Jerry offered no resistance to my request and immediately understood why.

For me, what is common to George D and Jerry and all the men I've loved is their non-transactional generosity of spirit and—beyond their many achievements—their capacity to laugh at themselves. That, dear reader, is my *sine qua non*.

NOTE FROM THE AUTHOR

O N MY RETIREMENT from Hunter in 2015, and to my utter surprise, I received an unexpected kudo in being awarded an honorary professorship in medicine, dentistry, and social work at the University of Melbourne. That took eight months of bureaucratic wrangling and hurt antipodal feelings to undo. In addition to the honour (sic) itself, it offered free access to the Uni Library, a free email account, and a free university parking space anytime I was in Melbourne. However, these perks meant giving up the possibility of serving as an external examiner on PhD dissertations, something I still cherish there and anywhere that will have me.

In 1994, however, I did gratefully accept an invitation to be the first social work academic ever invited to give the Miegunyah Distinguished Visiting Fellow Lecture at the University of Melbourne. That award changed my life in profoundly positive ways.

Coincidentally, in my public lecture, I revealed that the author of *Kangaroo* was not D.H. Lawrence at all, but the noted plagiarist Lawrence H. Davison, which I later discovered was Lawrence's other pen name. It caused quite a stir but began a long, beautiful, and productive collaboration with Aussies that lasted decades.

When I approached my editor at Oxford University Press with the idea for this uncharacteristic, non-academic book, he rejected it as "too memoirish." Soon after, learning of this rejection, my dear friend Professor Annie Pirrie of the University of North West Scotland, found in an Edinburgh thrift shop an OUP-published memoir entitled *Avoid Boring People: Lessons from a Life in*

Science written by the Nobel Prize-winning scientist James Watson published in 2007. Noting this, I returned to my OUP editor in New York and pointed out this contradiction.

He replied that it was published by OUP in the UK, not the USA, and besides, I hadn't won a Nobel Prize. To which I replied, just as Jerry did to me, "There's still time."

In 2021, I virtually attended the International Conference on Social Work Research in Beijing where Professor Ku Hok Bun (Ben) of the Hong Kong Polytechnic University was the discussant who responded to a plenary speech given by me.

Simultaneously translated into Chinese, Russian, and Vietnamese, the talk concerned Aristotle's tripartite typology of friendship as described and updated by the living Greek philosopher Alexander Nehamas, currently teaching in the philosophy department at Princeton. In my talk, I proposed that the ideal relationship between research and practice in social work be a *virtue friendship*.

Looking back but not bothering to test the empirical veracity of this statement, my guess is that the word *virtue* never appears in this book. Virtue is a Platonic ideal for gods and philosophers, not for living men or women.

Though Nehamas does importantly add the modern concepts of *friends with benefits* and *frenemies* to Aristotle's typology, his descriptions of his close friendships are less intimate, self-revealing, and funny or sad as mine. Such is the abstract and otherworld nature of philosophy.

My new Hong Kong friend Ben's Zoom response to the plenary was so thoughtful, intelligent, penetrating, empathic, and witty that while I was listening and mentally preparing my response to his, the thought intruded, *Hey, this guy could be my friend!*

And now we are, exchanging thoughts about culture (Ben is a cultural anthropologist), religion, food (with pictures), pedagogy, and personal history. We do this via email. We never talk politics (who knows who is listening?) but nothing else is off our kitchen table. I know about his late father and his living mother. I requested pictures of the Christmas dinner he cooked for his graduate students, knowing that his mother was of Hakka ethnicity. I was disappointed to see an enormous, beautifully glazed roast turkey and baked sweet potatoes (sans marshmallows). *Where do you buy a twenty-five-pound turkey in Hong Kong?* I wondered. *Why would you? Was it kosher?*

I wanted to see Hakka dishes. He explained, "My students see Chinese food all the time. I wanted to give them an experience of an American Christmas dinner!" Who am I to argue?

But the lesson here isn't what to serve at Christmas, Chanukah, or Kwanza, it's as you grow old, keep making friends. The more diverse in age and everything else, the better.

Of course, in my life there are and have always been loving women friends as well. I won't name them, but I assure you they know who they are. How do they know? I tell them every chance I get.

Still, this book is for men, however they arrived there, and for the women, by whatever provenance, who care to love them.

ACKNOWLEDGMENTS

F OR THOSE WORRYING about whether Jerry is my only remaining male friend, making me ever more vulnerable should he predecease, he promised he would not. But Jerry and those I've lost are only part of my life.

By employing Occam's razor to limit almost all of my stories to dear friends I have lost, there are several men of varying ages and descriptions, sexual orientations, and ethnicities who remain quite alive to my great delight and continue to enrich my life enormously. These include: Mike Austin, Zenon Bankowski, Ted Benjamin, Joe Boskin, Michael Bramwell, Andrew Bruun, Wallace Chan, Jimmy Fogarty, Allen Frances, Fritz Gaenslen, Bruce Gantt, Jeffrey Harper, Craig Hodges, Jerrold Jackson, Aamir Jamal, Jacques Joubert, Marc Klein, Nicholas Liu, Herman Lo, Nicholas Luis, Dana Holman, Dan Hughes, Steve Kapp, Paul Neitman, Siu-man Ng, Sam Poston, Ben Sheppard, David Stadleman, Tony Stakis, Chris Tanti, Bruce Thyer, Martin Webber, Stanley Yancovitz and preternaturally out of order, Lars Uggerhøj—the Danish herring and cheese denier.

Next to Jerry, Leonard Quart is my oldest living friend. I have urged him not to die before the book is published so I won't have to re-write about him. Lenny is a literary and film critic, and should he predecease publication of this book he would no doubt return to read what I have written about him and to honestly and acutely critique it. To guard against the inevitable possibility of a posthumously written review by Quart, I've asked him to submit a list of his many positive qualities which he is currently compiling. It might take a while. Humility is near the top. There are, of course, no negatives.

A special mention goes to a relatively new but nonetheless dear friend George Roper, whose blandishments to be included I've had to forcefully repel. Writing about him deceased solely because George IV is his favorite English King is too great a literary price for me to pay for his inclusion. I have my standards.

I thank my wife, Fran, for encouraging me to find a new project in my retirement and making the space in her hyper-medicalized and decreasingly active social life for me to write it. She has graced me with her charming company, love of life, and sense of adventure through thirty-two years of marriage, almost all those years living with cancer as an uninvited guest. She is my hero of heroes.

Special thanks to my children, Dan and Becs and Fran's daughter Molly, who have put up with me and my weird ways for decades, and my loving sister, Carole, who didn't flinch about my writing a memoir including our father, but for completely understandable reasons, won't read it. Tolstoy was right.

And thanks to my splendid editor, Nicki Wheir, who said "go for it" and went with me and my quirky book all the way. That was an absolute joyride. To the guys at Koehler Books—John and Joe—who became friends of a different sort and especially to Danielle Koehler for her brilliantly evocative cover design.

Finally, I want to thank Annie Pirrie my "epistemological virtue friend" who got me thinking about writing about friendship in the first place.

ABOUT THE AUTHOR

I RWIN EPSTEIN IS currently professor emeritus at Silberman School of Social Work, Hunter College of the City University of New York where he taught for thirty-five years. Prior to that, he taught at the University of Michigan School of Social Work from 1968-1980. In 1971, he was awarded a Fulbright-Hays Senior Lectureship to the University of Wales (Cardiff). At Hunter, in 2005, he became the first occupant of the Helen Rehr Chair in Applied Social Work Research in Health and Mental Health, in whose honor he proudly served for twenty years both nationally and internationally. In 2008, he was named to the Columbia University School of Social Work's Hall of Fame. He officially retired in 2015.

He lives in New York City with his wife, Fran.